Little Learning Labs

ASTRONOMY FOR KIDS

26 Family-Friendly Activities to Explore Stars, Planets, and Observing the World Around You

QUARRY

MICHELLE NICHOLS

Brimming with creative inspiration, how-to projects, and useful information to enrich your everyday life, Quarto Knows is a favorite destination for those pursuing their interests and passions. Visit our site and dig deeper with our books into your area of interest: Quarto Creates, Quarto Cooks, Quarto Homes, Quarto Lives, Quarto Drives, Quarto Explores, Quarto Gifts, or Quarto Kids.

First Published in 2018 by Quarry Books, an imprint of The Quarto Group,
100 Cummings Center, Suite 265-D, Beverly, MA 01915, USA.
T (978) 282-9590 F (978) 283-2742 QuartoKnows.com

Quarry Books titles are also available at discount for retail, wholesale, promotional, and bulk purchase. For details, contact the Special Sales Manager by email at specialsales@quarto.com or by mail at The Quarto Group, Attn: Special Sales Manager, 401 Second Avenue North, Suite 310, Minneapolis, MN 55401, USA.

10 9 8 7 6 5 4 3 2 1

ISBN: 978-1-63159-560-8

Digital edition published in 2018
The content in this book originally appeared in the book *Astronomy Lab for Kids* (Quarry Books, 2016).

Design and Page Layout: Marie-Anne Verougstraete
Illustrations: Shutterstock
Photography: David Miller, Miller Visual

Printed in China

I would like to dedicate this book to the following people:

First and foremost, my parents, who always encouraged me to reach for the stars in everything I have ever done

My family and friends, who never, ever said, "No, you shouldn't do that," and especially my brother Mark who is as geeked-out about science as I am

And last, but never least, my husband, Brian, who has been my number-one fan

Thank you, all. You have inspired me and encouraged me more than you will ever know.

Contents

Introduction

As far back as I can remember, I have observed the sky. One of my earliest memories is of riding in the back of my parents' car, looking out the window, and exclaiming, "URFO, URFO!" *URFO* was my five-year-old way of pointing out something I couldn't identify . . . something flashing, something moving against a background of twinkly things that weren't flashing or moving as quickly. It also may very well have been a conglomeration of seeing airplanes and watching *Close Encounters of the Third Kind* a few too many times. No matter. If there was something flying in the sky that I couldn't identify, it was a UFO—or, rather, a URFO. More importantly, searching for these things got me in the habit of looking up.

The night sky of my hometown was amazing. Back then, it was still dark enough that we could see the Milky Way from our backyard. Many a summer Saturday night was spent popping popcorn, watching the sky, and pointing our small telescope at whatever we could find. I even had a homemade observing kit containing my handwritten notebook, my binoculars, my constellation finder wheel, and my astronomy guide. In my notebook, I drew the stars of the Big Dipper. I learned how to find objects in the sky. I sketched the Moon. One image, though, is seared into my memory: the very first time I ever saw Saturn through our telescope. It was amazing! I could see the rings! Saturn became more than just a picture on television or in a book. It became *a place, a world* to observe and explore. Astronomy became very real for me from then onward. I wanted to learn more.

This drive to learn and know still inspires me today to help connect children and adults to the sky above us. As a museum educator for more than twenty years, my primary job has been to help people figure out what's out there and how it all works. I want everyone to understand that no expensive equipment is required to begin to investigate the world—and worlds—around us. The Universe is an amazing place to explore. Just bring your curiosity and your wonder . . . and don't forget to look up!

The Hubble Space Telescope captured light from about two million stars in the cluster called Omega Centauri.

Credit: NASA, ESA, and the Hubble Heritage Team (STScI/AURA)

Overview

A variety of activities is contained in this book. Many can be done in one sitting, but others require observations over a few hours, a few days, or even a few months, depending on what you are investigating. You probably have many of the materials needed around your house already, and others that you may not have are simple to obtain. I also recommend that you start keeping a science journal or notebook to record your observations, results, questions, comments, and drawings. This will help you, especially for those activities that take longer periods of time to complete or that require several sessions.

Each lab contains an easy-to-understand explanation of the vocabulary and ideas you will explore, and each contains the following sections:

→ **Time** shows you approximately how long it will take to complete all the steps.

→ **Materials** lists all the items you'll need to conduct each lab.

→ **Safety Tips and Setup Hints** gives you common-sense guidelines to make your investigations as safe and enjoyable as possible and highlights some steps to do in advance, if needed.

→ **Instructions** takes you step by step through a lab.

→ **The Science Behind the Fun** offers digestible explanations for each lab.

→ **Creative Enrichment** gives you variations or ideas for taking the project a step or two further.

Hopefully, you'll be inspired to come up with some additional ideas of your own.

This book contains activities that are tried, true, and tested, and they will help you begin to make sense of the Sun, Moon, planets, and stars. Several of the tools created for some of the earlier activities will be used in later ones. One thing this book is not, however, is an encyclopedia of everything you ever wanted to know about astronomy. That would be too much for one book! More Resources (see page 74) gives you some suggestions for taking advantage of stellar astronomy resources online and in your community to extend your explorations even further.

Parents, this book is as much for you as it is for your children. Help them with concepts and vocabulary, and assist with the activities where you can. Hopefully, everyone will learn something new.

Please keep in mind throughout your investigations that science is more than just the results of an experiment or activity. Science is messy and fun. Scientists ask questions, such as *why, how, what, where, and when*—as we all do! Science is about answering questions and then asking a hundred more. Science is not just about finding the "right" answer; scientists learn just as much from their failures as their successes. Science is wonder and science is discovery; so together, let's wonder about and discover more about our place in the Universe!

Science Journal

Scientists keep personal notebooks to document and detail background research, experiments, interesting results, thoughts, ideas, and questions. Some keep paper notebooks and others keep electronic ones. Why do they do this? Shouldn't they be spending their time doing experiments?

While experiments are important to many scientists, one of the most important skills for a scientist to practice is the ability to communicate ideas to an audience. A fantastic experiment with wonderful results means nothing if you can't explain to someone else what happened. There are several reasons for honing these skills. First, a scientist wants others to know the results of an experiment or the progress that has been made in researching something new. Secondly, a scientist wants others to be able to *replicate* the same experiment that was performed, meaning another person or team should be able to follow the experiment instructions to repeat them to confirm (or disprove!) the results. Thirdly, science is usually done by teams of men and women working together, not by individuals working completely alone. It is important for the team members to communicate well with one another so everyone can keep up with what everyone else is doing. Finally, some experiments may take a very long time to complete, and it would be extremely difficult to remember what happened months or years earlier if notes weren't kept all along the way.

Your family can practice keeping your own individual science notebooks as you do the activities in this book. Here is a sample format you may want to follow.

Name: your name

Date: today's date

What I Will Do: a quick summary of the lab you are going to do, in your own words

My Questions: questions you have about the activity before you start

My Materials: the materials you plan to use in the lab

My Observations: observations you make during the lab; what you see, hear, touch

My Data: the information, or data, you collect during the lab; don't forget to label your units—weights, lengths, times, and so on.

My Reflections: your feelings about how you think the lab went, what you think the lab results mean, and any answers to your questions you have found

My Concerns: any issues or problems you encountered, plus any solutions you came up with

Is it okay to include artwork if you would rather draw than write? Of course it is! Use any format you are comfortable with that helps you keep track of what you are doing. Remember, there is no single "correct" format. Use what works best for you.

After you've completed one of the activities in this book, think of other ways you could address the same ideas. Try some of the enrichment activities or invent a new way to do the same lab. How can what you have learned be applied to the world around you? Write down your thoughts in your notebook so you can come back to them in the future.

Observing

Often in school, we are told to "observe something." Observe this experiment. Observe what happens when a liquid is added to a powder. But what does it *mean* to observe? Am I just supposed to watch something happen? How do I know what to look for?

The skill of observation involves much more than just pointing your eyes in the direction of something. Observing is an *active* experience utilizing your senses of touch, smell, sight, taste, and hearing. Observing also involves using instruments to extend your senses and recording information from your observations.

The following activities will get your senses rolling—from observing angles in the sky, directions, and apparent motions of the Sun, to observations that can tell you about twinkling stars, the color of the Sun, and the phases of the Moon. Let's start practicing our skills of observation by using our senses and simple materials.

This view of the Full Moon was taken by NASA's *Clementine* spacecraft in 1994.
Credit: NASA/Goddard Space Flight Center Scientific Visualization Studio

LAB 01

Making Observations

Time

10 minutes

Materials

- Paper lunch bag, pillowcase, reusable grocery bag, or any other opaque bag
- Small items from around the house with interesting textures, shapes, or materials
- Your science notebook
- Pencil

Safety Tips and Setup Hints

- The more interesting items you choose for this lab, the better! However, **be very careful that your items do not contain sharp edges, pointy pieces, or have materials that are dangerous to touch, smell, or handle**. Do not choose objects that are especially warm or cold.

How do I observe if I can't see? Use your other senses!

Instructions

Step 1: Choose who will be the Leader and who will be the Observer.

Step 2: Leader, place one item in the bag without the Observer seeing what you have selected.

Observer, use your senses of touch, smell, and hearing as you carefully reach into the bag and touch the item, pick it up, carefully shake it, smell it, but do not look into the bag at all. If you need to pull the item out of the bag to make your observations, close your eyes so you do not see it. (Fig. 1)

Step 3: Observer, tell the Leader what you notice about the item. What does it feel like? What is it made of? Is it heavy or light? Does it have an odor? Is it smooth or rough? Is it made of metal, wood, plastic, fabric, or more than one material? How big is it? Does it remind you of something else? Is it made of parts or is it one piece? Does it make a sound when you move or shake it? Does it feel warm or cool? As you make your various observations, say them aloud.

Leader, as the Observer makes his or her observations, write them in your science notebook. (Fig. 2)

Step 4: Observer, once you have made all your initial observations, use your sense of sight to look at the object. What color is it? Is it shiny or dull? Is it transparent, translucent, or opaque?

Leader, record the observations made by the Observer. Finally, draw sketches of the object from the top or bottom, from the side, or from close-up or far away. (Fig. 3) ◆

The Science Behind the Fun

Did you notice the goal of this lab is not to try to guess what the item in the bag actually is? You could do that, if you wanted to, but the main goal was to involve *all* your senses to determine different scientific characteristics of an object, such as its length, width, height, weight, what it is made of, its sounds, and smells, how it moves (or doesn't move), and more. Only after figuring out everything you could without looking at it could you actually use your sense of sight to fill in the blanks this sense could tell you, such as the color of an object or whether it was shiny. Sketching an object is also a very important scientific step, as seeing something from different viewpoints can tell you about how the object works, what its pieces do, or how it changes over time. Making complete observations with as many details as possible can tell you a lot about an object, and making good observations is a very important part of science—especially astronomy!

Creative Enrichment

Take your notebook and a pencil into a park, field, or forest. Find a comfortable spot where you can sit for a while. Make observations of what you see, hear, smell, and touch. Sketch the scene in front of you and to your right or left. Try to go to the same location in summer, fall, winter, and spring and repeat your observations. How does that place change over time? Record all your observations in your notebook.

Take your notebook and a pencil outside at night. Look at the Moon or the stars. Make observations of what you see, but also don't forget to observe the scene around you. Record as many details as you can. Go out a few days, weeks, or months later and repeat your observations as often as you can. Is the sky starting to become a little more familiar to you?

Fig. 1: Place an object in the bag.

Fig. 2: Is the object big? Small? Heavy? Light? Rough? Smooth?

Fig. 3: Use your sense of sight to make your observations complete. Light? Rough? Smooth?

Angles in Your Hands

Time

5 minutes

✂ ## Materials

- Your hands

Safety Tips and Setup Hints

- To find angles properly, make sure your arm is fully stretched out. Keep your elbow and your arm straight.

How far apart are objects in the sky? Use your simplest—and best!—tools to figure it out: your hands!

Instructions

Step 1: Stretch out your arm and stick out only your pinky (smallest) finger. The rest of your fingers should be closed. Find something off in the distance to compare to the size of the end of your pinky finger. Look down your arm at your pinky. The angle made by one side of your pinky finger to the other is one degree. If you are looking at something in the distance and it exactly matches the size of just the end of your outstretched pinky, we can say that object is one degree wide or tall. (Fig. 1)

Step 2: Stretch out your thumb. The angle made by one side of your thumb to the other is two degrees, so something off in the distance that is the same size as the end of your thumb is two degrees wide or tall. (Fig. 2)

Step 3: Stretch out your arm and make a closed fist. Hold your fist straight outward. The angle from the bottom of your pinky finger to the top of your index finger is about ten degrees. The angles made by your pinky (one degree), thumb (two degrees), and closed fist (ten degrees) are the angles you probably will use most often when observing the sky. (Fig. 3)

Fig. 1: The width of one pinky equals one degree.

Fig. 2: The width of one thumb equals two degrees.

Step 4: There are a few other angles you might find useful. Stretch out your middle three fingers so those fingers touch. The angle from one edge of your index finger to the outer edge of your ring finger is about five degrees. Next, stretch out your hand so your index finger and pinky finger are angled outward. The angle between your two fingers is about fifteen degrees. Finally, stretch out your hand so your pinky finger and thumb are angled outward. The angle between your thumb and pinky is about twenty-five degrees.

Step 5: Go outside to a place where you can see at least part of the horizon in the distance and the sky up over your head. Make a fist and stretch it out so the bottom of your fist meets the horizon. From the bottom of your fist to the top is equal to ten degrees. If you put one fist on top of the other all the way up to the top of the sky, how many fists do you need to reach directly above your head? It should be nine. Nine fists of ten degrees each equal ninety degrees. This point straight up in the sky has a special name. It is called the "zenith." The point opposite the zenith, straight down to the ground directly under your feet, is called the "nadir." The sky looks like a bowl up over your head down to the horizon on the ground. That much sky is half of a circle, or 180 degrees. ◆

Fig. 3: The height of one fist equals ten degrees.

The Science Behind the Fun

Draw a circle. If you draw a line down the middle of the circle from top to bottom, you now have divided the circle into two equal pieces. If you add a line across the middle going from the left side of the circle to the right side, you now have four equal pieces. Another way to divide the circle is to draw 180 lines so you end up with 360 little pie shapes that are all the same size. Each rounded edge along the edge of the circle is equal to 1 degree. The length of ten of those small rounded edges put together is equal to ten degrees of distance. One-half of a circle is 180 degrees, and one full circle equals 360 degrees.

Scientists use degrees to indicate how far apart objects appear in the sky. In many cases, though, one degree is still too large to describe how far apart objects are. For those small angles, they also divide each degree into even smaller pieces.

Creative Enrichment

Have you ever noticed how large the Moon appears to be when it is close to the horizon? Compare the size of the Moon to the width of your pinky (smallest) finger or your thumb when the Moon is close to the horizon. A few hours later, go outside and measure the Moon's width compared to the same finger when the Moon is a lot higher in the sky. Is this size difference real or is it an optical illusion?

Determining Directions

Time

20 minutes

Materials

- 1 thin stick about 12 inches (30 cm) long
- 2 more straight sticks about 12 to 18 inches (30 to 45 cm) long
- 1 ball of clay about 3 inches (8 cm) in diameter
- 2 small rocks or other small objects
- 4 pieces of paper; mark the first with N, the second with S, the third with E, and the fourth with W

Safety Tips and Setup Hints

- You'll need a fairly sunny day for this lab, but a day with some clouds may work, too.
- **Never look directly at the Sun!** Doing so may *very quickly* cause eye damage or blindness.
- Choose an observation spot that is fairly flat and clear of large objects, such as trees or fences, which might cast shadows on it.

Use the Sun and some simple materials to find the cardinal directions: north, south, east, and west.

Instructions

Step 1: Start this lab around midday. The exact time does not matter.

Step 2: Push the end of the 12-inch (30 cm) stick into the ground. If your observation spot is on a hard surface, press the end of your stick into the ball of clay to hold it upright. If the stick doesn't stand up by itself, add a little more clay.

Step 3: Look for the shadow of the stick on the ground. Mark the end of the shadow with a small object, such as a rock. (Fig. 1)

Fig. 1: Mark your first shadow spot.

Fig. 2: Mark your second shadow point.

Fig. 3: Determine your east-west line.

Step 4: In about fifteen minutes, mark the shadow again with another small rock. (Fig. 2)

Step 5: Line up your second stick with the two rocks. This is your east-west line. West is in the direction of your first measurement point. East is in the direction of your second measurement point. Put the E and W signs at the correct ends of the stick. (Fig. 3)

Step 6: Place the third stick perpendicular to your east-west stick. This is your north-south line. Face your east-west stick so east is on your right. North will be ahead of you, and south will be to your back. Put your N and S labels on the ground next to the north-south stick. You have found your directions! (Fig. 4)

Step 7: Look around and find landmarks to help you locate the cardinal directions again from this spot in the future. Make notes in your notebook to record your findings. ◆

The Science Behind the Fun

The Earth spins, or rotates, but to a viewer standing on the rotating Earth, the Earth seems to stand still and the Sun appears to rise, travel across the sky, and set. As the Sun appears to move, shadows cast by the Sun also move. We can use these shadow movements to tell us where our directions are.

Of course, you can find your directions with a compass or a GPS-enabled device, such as a smartphone. But what if you don't have either of these tools or your batteries run out? The two-point stick method will work without any technology at all!

Creative Enrichment

Do the streets in your neighborhood line up with the cardinal directions?

Has anyone ever told you the appearance of moss on a tree can help you find your directions? Use your direction information and make some observations of several trees in your area. Record your findings in your notebook. Is this really true?

Fig. 4: Success! You found all four directions!

◆

LAB 04

Sunrise, Sunset

Time

5 to 15 minutes per observation, with observations spread throughout the year

Materials

- Your science notebook
- Pencil

Safety Tips and Setup Hints

- **Never look directly at the Sun!** Doing so may *very quickly* cause eye damage or blindness.
- The time of sunrise or sunset may be found in a variety of places, such as in your local newspaper's weather section, the weather portion of your local TV newscast, or online at the U.S. Naval Observatory's website: aa.usno.navy.mil/data/docs/RS_OneDay.php.

Does the Sun always rise in the east and set in the west? Let's find out!

Instructions

Step 1: After learning how to determine east and west in Lab 3, "Determining Directions" (see page 18), choose a spot where you can see to the east or west all the way to the horizon (ideally, a place where you can see both directions). In your notebook, sketch what you see on the horizon to the east and west. Include details, such as buildings, houses, trees, bushes, or any other landmarks. Make sure you can use this same observation site and see the same landmarks each time you do this lab. (Fig. 1)

Step 2: Go to your observation spot about five minutes before sunrise or about five minutes before sunset. Watch for sunrise or sunset and note the location on the horizon where sunrise or sunset occurred. Write the date and time in your notebook to correspond with your observation. Ideally, record the position of sunrise and sunset on the same day, though this may depend on the weather. If you miss a sunrise or sunset observation on the same day, you can go out a day or two later. (Fig. 2)

Step 3: Do these observations for a year and record your data. You can go out once every few days, every few weeks, once per month, or once every couple of months.

The most important dates to observe are on or near December 21, March 21, June 21, and September 22.

Step 4: When you have completed your observations, analyze the data in your notebook. Does the Sun appear to rise directly in the east every day? Does it appear to set directly in the west every day? ◆

Fig. 1: Record data about your observation spot.

The Science Behind the Fun

The positions of sunrise and sunset change throughout the year because the Earth's axis is tilted. The Earth's axis is the imaginary line running from the North Pole to the South Pole directly through the center of the Earth. If the Earth stood straight up and down on its axis, the Sun would appear to rise directly east and set directly west every day. However, because the Earth's axis is tilted at 23.5 degrees and the Earth revolves around the Sun, the positions of sunrise and sunset change throughout the year. The Sun appears to rise directly east and set directly west only on two dates during the year, the spring and fall equinoxes in March and September. How far the positions of sunrise and sunset stray directly from east and west depends on the latitude—the distance north or south of the equator—of the observer.

Creative Enrichment

Do you know someone who lives in another city or country? On or near the same dates, do some sunrise and sunset observations and compare your data. Record the latitude of both of your locations. What similarities and differences do you notice?

To find your latitude, use NASA's Latitude/Longitude Finder: mynasadata.larc.nasa.gov/latitudelongitude-finder

Fig. 2: Where does the Sun appear to rise? Where does it appear to set?

Time

5 to 10 minutes per observation, once per month for a year

Materials

- Ruler or measuring tape
- Your science notebook
- Pencil

Safety Tips and Setup Hints

- You'll need a fairly sunny day for this lab, but a day with some clouds may work, too.
- **Never look directly at the Sun!** Doing so may *very quickly* cause eye damage or blindness.
- You'll need a flat surface for this lab, such as a sidewalk or a driveway.
- The lab requires two people, the "Shadow Maker" and the "Measurement Maker." The Shadow Maker should stand in the same spot facing the same direction each time a measurement is made.
- If you are interested in knowing your latitude, use NASA's Latitude/Longitude Finder: mynasadata.larc.nasa.gov/latitudelongitude-finder

At "local noon," does the Sun appear directly overhead where you live?

Fig. 1: Find the time of local noon.

Fig. 2: Measure the length of the Shadow Maker's shadow.

Instructions

Step 1: You will need to do this lab when the Sun is highest in the sky, also called "local noon." To find the time of local noon in your area, go to the U.S. Naval Observatory's website, aa.usno.navy.mil/data/docs/RS_OneDay.php, and enter the date you will do your observation and your location in the form fields. Click the "Get Data" button. On the page that comes up, look for the time of "Sun transit." This is the time the Sun appears highest in the sky where you are located, also called "local noon." (Fig. 1)

Step 2: A few minutes before the time of Sun transit, go to your observation spot. At the time of Sun transit, the Shadow Maker should stand tall and face south. The Measurement Maker will measure the length of the shadow from the Shadow Maker's feet to the end of the longest point on the shadow, which will be the shadow cast by the Shadow Maker's head. Record this shadow length in your science notebook, along with the date and time. (Fig. 2)

Step 3: Repeat these steps about once per month, using the same person as the Shadow Maker each time. The key date to make your observation is the first day of summer, called the "summer solstice." In the Northern Hemisphere, this is around June 21 each year. In the Southern Hemisphere, it is around December 21 each year. Try to make your shadow length observation on the solstice, though doing so a few days before or after will be fine. (Fig. 3)

Step 4: Analyze your data. If the Sun is directly overhead at your spot at some point during the year, you will see the Shadow Maker has cast no extended shadow. In other words, the shadow length will be zero, and the shadow would be right at the Shadow Maker's feet. Is the Sun directly overhead at your location? ◆

Fig. 3: Head out to measure your shadow around the first day of summer.

The Science Behind the Fun

Because the Earth's axis is tilted at 23.5 degrees, for latitudes between 23.5 degrees north and 23.5 degrees south, the Sun appears directly overhead at some point during the year. For the latitude of 23.5 degrees north, the Sun appears directly overhead at the Northern Hemisphere summer solstice on or near June 20 or June 21. For the latitude of 23.5 degrees south, the Sun appears directly overhead at the Southern Hemisphere summer solstice, which is on or near December 21 or 22. There are special names for these special latitudes: 23.5 degrees north latitude is known as the Tropic of Cancer, and 23.5 degrees south latitude is known as the Tropic of Capricorn. For all latitudes north of 23.5 degrees north and all latitudes south of 23.5 degrees south, the Sun never appears directly overhead. It might look close to being overhead, but it isn't!

Creative Enrichment

Do you know someone who lives in another city or country? On or near the same dates, do your shadow length observations and compare your data. Record the latitude of both of your locations. What do you notice?

Our Colorful Sun

⏱ Time

20 minutes

✂ Materials

- 1 small ball of white play dough, play clay, or air-dry clay
- 1 (10-inch, or 25 cm) clear hot melt glue stick cut into 2 pieces (see Setup Hint)
- Duct tape
- 1 piece of cardboard 8 inches (20 cm) on a side
- Small white LED flashlight, ideally with a light about the same size as the glue stick

Safety Tips and Setup Hints

- An adult will need to use a sharp blade to cut the hot melt glue stick. One piece should be about 1 inch (2.5 cm) long, and the other piece should be about 4 inches (10 cm) long.
- Shape the small ball of play dough into a cube the same width as the glue stick. Let the cube sit out for a while until it is dry.

Our Sun is yellow, right? Are you sure? Seeing can be deceiving.

Fig. 1: Fasten your clay cube to the cardboard.

Fig. 2: Attach the glue stick pieces to the cardboard.

Instructions

Step 1: Attach the clay cube in the center of the piece of cardboard with duct tape. (Fig. 1)

Step 2: Attach the shorter glue stick piece so it sits about ½ inch (1 cm) above the top of your cube. Attach the longer glue stick piece about ½ inch (1 cm) to the right of the cube. (Fig. 2)

Step 3: Turn on the flashlight and turn off the lights in the room. Notice the color of the light coming from the flashlight. Now, hold the flashlight up against the small glue stick piece so light shines on the cube. What color is the light shining on the cube? (Fig. 3)

Step 4: Hold the flashlight up against the longer glue stick piece so the light shines on the cube. What color is the light shining on the cube? (Fig. 4) ◆

Fig. 3: See the color of the light shining through the small glue stick?

Fig. 4: Is the color of the light shining through the longer glue stick the same?

The Science Behind the Fun

Have you seen a rainbow? What colors did you see? These are the colors that make up the light from our Sun. The light our eyes can detect is called "visible light." When all the light from all these colors is viewed together, the light from the Sun appears white. We also call this visible light "white light."

When the Sun's light hits air high up in our atmosphere, the air scatters the blue light. This blue light is what we see from the ground as a blue-colored sky. Because the blue light from the Sun is scattered, our Sun looks more yellow because this blue light has been, basically, "removed." When the Sun is really low in the sky, sunlight passes through even more air and scatters even more of the blue light from the Sun, leaving mostlyorange and red light. This leaves our Sun looking redder.

In this lab, the shorter glue stick represents the air above us and the longer glue stick represents the air toward the horizon. The shorter piece scatters blue light from the flashlight, making the light on the cube look a little more yellow. The longer piece scatters even more blue light, making the light on the cube look a little redder. So, what color is our Sun? Is it yellow? Orange? Red? The flashlight gives us the best clue. Depending on how much glue stick the white light passed through, the light at the end appeared different, but the white light from the flashlight itself didn't change. Our Sun really is white! If you were an astronaut in space, the Sun would look white.

Creative Enrichment

Japan is called the "land of the rising Sun." What color does the rising Sun appear to be? What is the object depicted on the national flag of Japan? Create a collage of other flags of the world that depict the Sun and research the stories behind the use of the Sun in those flags.

Our Changing Moon

Time

10 minutes

Materials

- Chair
- 1 bright lamp with the shade removed or a flashlight
- 1 round, white polystyrene ball at least 2 inches (5 cm) in diameter (your "Moon")
- Your science notebook
- Pencil

Safety Tips and Setup Hints

- This lab requires two people, one person to hold the ball, the "Modeler," and one person to make observations of the phases, the "Observer."
- Do not use Styrofoam balls for this lab; the rough texture of Styrofoam will make the line between the shadow and bright areas harder to see. Polystyrene balls should be available at craft stores.

(Continues on page 26)

Why does our Moon appear to be different shapes? Spin around and see!

Instructions

Step 1: Observer, place the chair in the middle of the room and sit in it. You represent someone standing on the Earth observing the Moon as it goes around you.

Modeler, hold the Moon ball away from you at the same height as the top of the Observer's head and do not let it fall lower than the Observer's eye level. Walk in a circle about 5 feet (1.5 m) from the Observer. (Fig. 1)

Step 2: Modeler, hold the Moon ball in between the Observer and the light.

Observer, look for the Moon ball. Do you see any of the lit part? No! This is the Moon phase called "New Moon." The Moon is in the same part of the sky as the Sun.

Step 3: Modeler, walk a short distance around the Observer in a counterclockwise circle.

Observer, tell the Modeler to stop when you see a small bit of the right side of the Moon ball lit by the lamp. This Moon phase is called "Crescent Moon." (Fig. 2)

Step 4: Modeler, walk a little farther.

Observer, tell the Modeler to stop when you see the right half of the Moon ball lit by the lamp. This Moon phase is called "First Quarter Moon." (Fig. 3)

(Continues on page 26)

Fig. 1: The Modeler walks the Moon ball around the Observer.

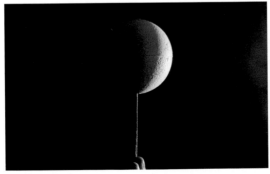

Fig. 2: See the little bit of light on the right side?

Fig. 3: This is First Quarter Moon.

Safety Tips and Setup Hints

(Continued from page 24)

- If the polystyrene ball does not have a small hole in the bottom, an adult should drill a hole just large enough so the pencil can fit. The pencil will be your handle.

- For this lab, use a room that can be completely darkened. Place the bright light at one end of the room.

Step 5: Modeler, walk a little more.

Observer, tell the Modeler to stop when you see most of the right side of the Moon ball lit by the lamp. This Moon phase is called "Gibbous Moon" (pronounced GIB-bus).

Step 6: Modeler, walk a little farther around the Observer.

Observer, tell the Modeler to stop when you see the entire side of the Moon ball facing you lit by the lamp. This Moon phase is called "Full Moon." (Fig. 4)

Step 7: Modeler, walk a little farther around the Observer.

Observer, tell the Modeler to stop when you see most of the left side of the Moon ball lit by the lamp. This is also a "Gibbous Moon."

Step 8: Modeler, keep going a little farther.

Observer, tell the Modeler to stop when you see the left half of the Moon ball lit by the lamp. This phase is called "Third Quarter Moon." (Fig. 5)

Step 9: Modeler, keep going in a circle.

Observer, tell the Modeler to stop when you see a sliver of the Moon ball on the left side lit by the lamp. This phase is also called a "Crescent Moon." (Fig. 6)

Step 10: Modeler, you should return to holding the Moon ball in the same part of the Observer's view as the lamp. This, again, is the New Moon. ✦

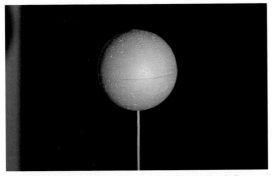
Fig. 4: Full Moon is when the Moon is opposite the Sun in the sky—as the Sun sets, the Full Moon rises.

Fig. 5: See the lit left half of the Moon ball?

Fig. 6: See the little bit of light on the left side?

The Science Behind the Fun

Just as the Earth moves around the Sun, our Moon orbits the Earth. Two other terms for "moves around" are "revolves around" or "orbits." The time it takes for the Moon to orbit the Earth once is approximately 29½ Earth days. In other words, the Earth spins 29½ times in the time it takes for the Moon to go around the Earth once. Half of the Moon is always lit by the Sun, and Moon phases are just the changing amount of the Moon that is lit by the Sun *as seen from Earth.*

Creative Enrichment

The name "dark side of the Moon" has been used by some people to describe the side of the Moon that faces away from the Earth. Is this an appropriate name? Why or why not?

Eclipse the Sun, Eclipse the Moon

Time

5 minutes

✂ Materials

- This lab uses the same materials as Lab 7, "Our Changing Moon" (see page 24), plus more in this list.
- Small white LED flashlight, such as a penlight flashlight. The flashlight used for Lab 6, "Our Colorful Sun" (see page 22), would work well, too.
- Very small ball of play dough or play clay, no larger than ½ inch (1 cm) in diameter

Safety Tips and Setup Hints

- Please follow the same "Safety Tips and Setup Hints" as Lab 7, "Our Changing Moon" (see page 24).
- Remember always to move the Moon ball in a *counterclockwise* direction around the Observer. This represents the direction the Moon orbits the Earth.

What is an eclipse? When can I see one?

Fig. 1: When the Sun is blocked by the Moon, this is a solar eclipse.

Instructions

Step 1: Modeler, hold the Moon ball so it is in the same part of the Observer's view as the lamp bulb, as you did for the phase known as New Moon. This time, try to block the light from the Sun lamp so the Observer cannot see the lamp bulb.

Observer, tell the Modeler when the light from the lamp is fully blocked by the Moon ball. When the Moon fully covers the Sun as seen from Earth, this is called a "total solar eclipse." Observer, work with the Modeler to find a spot when the Moon ball partly covers the lightbulb so you can see just a bit of the light coming from the lamp. When the Moon covers only part of the Sun as seen from Earth, this is called a "partial solar eclipse." (Fig. 1)

Fig. 2: During a lunar eclipse, the Moon appears darker. Fig. 3: Transits only cover a tiny part of the Sun.

Step 2: Modeler, hold the Moon ball as you did for the Full Moon phase, with the Moon ball on one side of the Observer and the lamp on the opposite side.

Observer, tell the Modeler when the Moon ball passes through the shadow cast by your head. When the Moon passes through the shadow cast by the Earth, this is called a "lunar eclipse." If the Moon partly passes through the Earth's shadow but the other part of it is still lit by the Sun, this is called a "partial lunar eclipse." If the Moon fully passes through the Earth's shadow, this is called a "total lunar eclipse." (Fig. 2)

Step 3: Modeler, put the Moon ball down and pick up the small ball of play clay. Stand about 5 feet (1.5 m) from the Observer. Move the ball so it passes between the Observer and the light, blocking a little bit of the light as seen by the Observer, but not all the light. When an object passes in front of the Sun but it is too small to cover the Sun completely, this is called a "transit." (Fig. 3) ◆

Creative Enrichment

The next time the planet Mercury will transit the Sun will be in 2019. See if this event will be visible in your area: aa.usno.navy.mil/data/docs/UpcomingTransits.php.

A few weeks before the transit, inquire if a local planetarium or astronomy club is planning to provide telescopes to see it. If so, check it out!

The Science Behind the Fun

An eclipse of the Sun occurs when the Moon passes between the Sun and an Observer on Earth. In our model, the Moon ball passed in front of the light, blocking it completely, and the shadow of the Moon ball fell on the Observer. These solar eclipses can occur only at the New Moon phase, when the Moon is in the same part of the sky as the Sun.

An eclipse of the Moon occurs when the Moon passes through the shadow cast by the Earth. In our model, the Moon ball passed through the shadow cast by the Observer's head. Lunar eclipses can only occur at the Full Moon phase, when the Moon is on the opposite side of the Earth as the Sun.

A "transit" occurs when an object passes between a star and an Observer, but the object does not completely cover and block all the light from the star. One of the more well-known transits is the Transit of Venus, when Venus passes between the Sun and the Earth. Venus can be seen as a small dot against the larger Sun. The last two Transits of Venus occurred in 2004 and 2012. The next one will be in 2117. Transits are also used by astronomers to find planets around other stars, as the distant planet blocks a tiny bit of light from its star. We see this effect as a temporary dimming of light from the star.

Twinkle, Twinkle

Time

10 minutes

Materials

- 1 clear glass bowl or container that holds at least 6 cups (1.5 liters) of liquid
- 4 cups (1 L) of cold water
- Small flashlight; the flashlight used for Lab 6, "Our Colorful Sun" (see page 22) would work well.
- 2 cups (500 ml) of warm water

Safety Tips and Setup Hints

- Use a darkened room for this lab.
- The twinkling effect will be more pronounced if the difference in temperature between the cold water and warm water is wider. Use hot tap water for the warm water, and put ice cubes into the cold water for a while. Be careful! The temperature of hot tap water is sometimes enough to cause burns.

Stars seem to twinkle, but why?

Instructions

Step 1: Pour the cold water into the bowl (without the ice cubes), and let the water settle so it is not moving. Don't fill up the bowl because you will need to pour more water in later. Turn on the flashlight and turn off the lights in the room. (Fig. 1)

Step 2: Point the flashlight at the bowl and bend down so you can see the light from the flashlight as you look through the side of the bowl and through the water. Place the flashlight about 12 inches (30 cm) from the bowl. Observe the light from the flashlight through the water. (Fig. 2)

Step 3: Slowly and carefully pour the warm water into the bowl, and again observe the light through the water. (It might help to have someone else pour the water for you.) What does pouring the warm water into the bowl do to the beam of light from the flashlight? (Fig. 3)

Step 4: This time, place the flashlight across the room at least 10 feet (3 m) from the bowl. Pour out all the water from the bowl. Replenish your amounts of cold and hot water and repeat the experiment. What do you notice about the beam of light when the flashlight is farther from the bowl? If you have room, keep repeating the experiment, moving the flashlight farther from the bowl each time. (Fig. 4)

Fig. 3: Pour the warm water in. What do you see?

Fig. 4: The light is farther away. Now what do you see?

Fig. 2: Observe the light as it goes through the water.

Fig. 1: Let the cold water settle in the bowl.

The Science Behind the Fun

When you go outside on a clear night, look up. Do you see stars? If so, watch them for a little while. What do you see? Chances are, if you watch long enough, the light from the stars will seem to wiggle or move a tiny bit. This is twinkling!

Stars are very large, but they are very, very far away, so they appear as tiny points in the sky. The tiny beam of light from a star passes through Earth's air to where you are standing on the ground. The air above you moves around a lot. It is this moving air that causes the beam of light to move around a bit.

Sometimes when you look at a twinkling star, it will appear to change color. Is the star actually changing color right before your eyes? No. A star's light contains all colors, from red, orange, and yellow to green, blue, and violet. Sometimes the colors of light from a star will twinkle differently, making the star appear to be one color, then another, and still another. This is especially easy to see with very bright stars viewed when they are closer to the horizon, as you are seeing them through more of Earth's air.

If you look at a star from space, will it twinkle? No! Because there is no air in space, there is nothing to cause the star's light to jiggle. The light from stars would appear steady if you saw them from space. This is why the Hubble Space Telescope has been such an amazing machine. It orbits above the blurring effects of Earth's air.

Creative Enrichment

When we look at planets in our Solar System from Earth, they do not seem to twinkle much at all. Why not? *Hint: How far away are planets in our Solar System compared to the stars we see at night?* Use an online star map or phone application to find when and where a planet, such as Venus, might be visible and compare its beam of light to that of a twinkling star.

Note: While this enrichment idea works for other planets such as Mercury, Mars, Jupiter, and Saturn, Venus will be the easiest object to spot because it will be brighter than anything else in the early morning or early evening sky—other than the Moon. If you don't know how to find planets in the sky, it is best to start practicing with Venus!

Scoping Out the Science

Many people think Galileo was the inventor of the telescope, but he was not. In 1608 Dutch lens makers were likely the first to do so. Galileo heard about this wonderful tool, and he worked to improve it. In 1609 he pointed his telescope at objects in the sky and kept a notebook of his observations.

Over many weeks and months, Galileo saw jagged mountains and craters on the Moon and phases of Venus that looked like phases of our Moon. He observed four objects that orbited the planet Jupiter, what we know to be Jupiter's four largest moons. He saw stars not visible to the naked eye, and more. In 1610 he published his observations in a book called *Starry Messenger*.

Telescopes seem complicated, don't they? Almost like magic, special lenses and mirrors show us things in the sky we didn't see before. It isn't magic, though. It's science! Let's use some simple materials to make these tools easier to understand.

On May 13, 2009, NASA astronauts on the space shuttle *Atlantis* captured this view of the Hubble Space Telescope against the backdrop of Earth.

Credit: NASA

Make a Pinhole Projector

⏱ Time

15 minutes

✂ Materials

- 1 long cardboard box (or more than one box taped together); the width and height are not particularly important, but the length should be at least 5 feet (1.5 m)
- Box cutter or a pair of very sharp, sturdy scissors
- 1 piece of aluminum foil about 6 inches (15 cm) on a side
- Pin, tack, or pushpin
- 1 sheet of white copy paper
- Masking tape, duct tape, or packing tape
- Small ruler (optional)

⛑ Safety Tips and Setup Hints

- You'll need a fairly sunny day for this lab.
- **Never look directly at the Sun,** and do not look through your pinhole or through your pinhole projector at the Sun! Doing so may *very quickly* cause eye damage or blindness.
- An adult should do any cutting using the scissors or box cutter. They can be extremely sharp.

Do you need a fancy camera to see an image of the Sun? No! Would you believe it's as easy as a pin?

Fig. 5: Point the pinhole at the Sun and look for an image on your screen.

Fig. 6: Here comes the Sun!

Instructions

Step 1: In the middle of one end of the box, measure a hole that is about 2 by 2 inches (5 by 5 cm) square. The hole does not have to be exactly in the middle of the end of the box, nor does the hole have to be exactly square. Cut out this hole and discard the piece you cut out. (Fig. 1)

Step 2: Securely tape the aluminum foil over the hole. Try to make the foil as smooth as possible. (Fig. 2)

Fig. 1: Cut the hole out of one end of the box.

Fig. 2: Tape aluminum foil over the hole.

Fig. 3: Punch a pinhole into the foil.

Step 3: Using the pin, carefully punch a small hole into the middle of the aluminum foil. Keep the hole the size of the pin itself. (Fig. 3)

Step 4: Opposite the pinhole end, cut open a flap in the side of the box and tape a sheet of white paper across the inside end of the box opposite the pinhole end. This is your "screen" where you will project the Sun's image. (Fig. 4)

Step 5: You can try out your pinhole projector inside using a bright lightbulb. Turn on the lightbulb, darken the room, point the pinhole end of the box at the lightbulb, and look for a small image of the bulb on the white sheet of paper. It may take a little practice. Don't get your head in the way!

Step 6: Once you are good at using your projector inside with lightbulbs, go outside and try to project an image of the Sun. You may find you will need to prop your box on a fence post, a deck railing, or some other sturdy object. Once you find the Sun successfully, it should get easier to do so repeatedly. (Figs. 5, 6) ◆

Fig. 4: Tape your "screen" inside the other end of your box.

The Science Behind the Fun

While everyone is probably most familiar with glass or plastic lenses as a way to make a sharp image of something, you can simply use a pinhole. The pinhole acts like a tiny lens, allowing an image of something bright to be seen at some distance from the pinhole.

You need a very long box for this lab. The size of the image of the Sun that the pinhole projects is only going to be about 1 percent of the length of the box. That means that for a box 60 inches (5 feet, or 1.5 m) in length, the image of the Sun the pinhole produces is only going to be 0.6 inches (1.5 cm) in diameter.

Creative Enrichment

When you look at the images of lightbulbs on your "screen," how are the images oriented? Are they right side up?

Try playing with several sizes of pinholes. What happens to the size or brightness of your image? Next, try changing the length of your projector box. If you keep your pinhole size the same but your projector box is longer or shorter, what happens to your image? Is there a "perfect" hole size for a certain length of projector box?

Detecting Infrared Light

Time
15 minutes

Materials
- Flat black paint or black permanent marker
- Alcohol thermometer
- Cardboard box
- Scissors or box cutter
- Glass prism
- 1 sheet of white copy paper
- Watch or timer

Safety Tips and Setup Hints
- Alcohol thermometers look like they have red-colored water in the bulb.
- Color the bulb of the thermometer with flat (not shiny) black paint or black permanent marker. Black paint works best, but if you do not have it, black marker will do. Let the paint or marker dry completely before you start.
- If your box has flaps on top, have an adult cut them off with the scissors or box cutter.

Use simple materials to detect something you can't see!

Instructions

Step 1: Cut a notch out of the top of one side of the box just big enough to hold the prism. You want the sides of the notch to hold the prism without you holding the prism with your hands. Put the prism into the notch. (Fig. 1)

Step 2: Put the sheet of paper on the bottom of the box. (Fig. 2)

Step 3: Go outside on a sunny day around noon or 1 p.m. in late spring, summer, or early autumn. Find a spot in the sun but out of the wind. Bring the box, the prism, thermometer, and timer. Turn the prism slowly until you see a rainbow on the bottom of the box. You may need to turn the box around to get the rainbow to appear on the bottom of the box. (Fig. 3)

Step 4: Put the thermometer somewhere nearby in the shade. Let it sit for a few minutes. Record the temperature on the thermometer.

Step 5: Look at the rainbow and see where the red end is. Put the thermometer just off the red end where it looks like there is no color. (Fig. 4)

Step 6: Let the thermometer sit in that part of the box for five to fifteen minutes (you may need to adjust the position of the box slightly to keep the rainbow in place, but do not let any of the rainbow touch the thermometer). At the end of the time, note the temperature on the thermometer again. What do you notice? ◆

Fig. 1: Slide the prism into the notch in the box.

Fig. 2: Put the paper in the box.

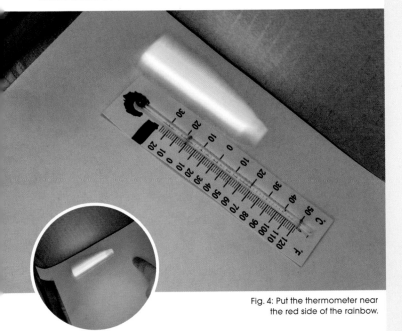

Fig. 4: Put the thermometer near the red side of the rainbow.

Fig. 3: Look for a rainbow in the box.

The Science Behind the Fun

In 1800 astronomer William Herschel was experimenting with the light from the Sun passing through his prism, and he noticed his thermometer recorded the highest temperature when it wasn't actually in the rainbow itself. The highest temperature he saw was just off the red end of the rainbow. He had discovered a form of light he couldn't see with his eyes. This light was called "infrared" (IN-fruh-RED). "Infra" in Latin means "below," so this was a form of light below the red end of the rainbow.

Infrared light is extremely useful. Infrared cameras are used to locate people and animals caught in thick smoke and for finding areas of forest that have burned where it looks like the fire is out, but are actually still hot enough to flare up and burn again. Infrared cameras are used to see where heat is escaping from buildings and wasting energy. Infrared telescopes see hidden things in space, too. Visible light cannot pass through dark dusty areas in space, but infrared light can, allowing us to see those stars that are normally hidden.

Creative Enrichment

This lab works best around midday, especially when the Sun is high in the sky. What happens to your results when you do this experiment early or late in the day? How about when the Sun is lower in the sky in early spring, late fall, or winter?

LAB 12

Make and Bake

Time

1 to 2 hours

Materials

- Clean, empty pizza box (from a medium-size pizza)
- Scissors or box cutter
- Aluminum foil
- Duct tape or clear packing tape
- 1 heavy gallon-size (3.4 L) zip-top bag
- Black paper
- 5 or 6 sheets of newspaper
- Clear glass or plastic plate (not paper)
- Graham crackers, chocolate, and marshmallows (for s'mores)

Safety Tips and Setup Hints

- If you need a clean pizza box, ask your local pizza shop for an extra box the next time you order a pizza. Tell them it's for science!
- This lab works best on a sunny day with very little wind. If it is windy, try to block your solar oven from the wind because wind might cool it down.

Making s'mores requires no fire at all—just a sunny day.

Instructions

Step 1: Flip the top of the pizza box up, and have an adult cut along three sides of the top to make a flap. Leave a 1-inch (2.5 cm) border around the edge of the box top. (Fig. 1)

Step 2: Pull the flap up, cover the inside of the flap with aluminum foil, and tape the foil onto the back of the flap.

Step 3: Cut the sides of the zip-top bag apart so you have two pieces of clear plastic. Cover the inside of the opening you cut into the box top with a sheet of plastic. Tape all sides of the plastic to the lid so no air can get through the sides.

Step 4: Cover the bottom of the pizza box with black paper and tape it down along the edges or by adding tape to the back of the paper. (Fig. 2)

Step 5: Roll sheets of newspaper into tubes and place them on the bottom of the box all along the edges of the box. Make sure you can still close the lid of the box. If you can't, make the rolls a little smaller. (Fig. 3)

Step 6: Take your solar cooker outside into the sunlight, and put it on a hard surface. Angle the aluminum foil flap until sunlight is passing through the clear plastic top into the cooker. Use a piece of cardboard or something sturdy to hold the flap at the right angle. You may also want to prop the box so the foil points directly at the Sun. (Fig. 4)

Fig. 1: Cut a flap in the box top.

Creative Enrichment

Test your solar oven by placing a cooking thermometer inside it that can show temperatures up to 200°F (about 93°C). Let your oven sit in the Sun for an hour or two. How hot does it get? Can you think of ways to make your solar oven even better? Can you angle more sunlight into the oven, change the design to get a hotter temperature, or make your oven bigger? Try new designs and see what works best! Remember, don't use magnifying glasses or any lenses that might set the paper or cardboard on fire. That would be too hot—and too dangerous!

Step 7: Put the food you want to cook onto a clear plastic or clear glass plate. For example, put a graham cracker on the plate and the chocolate on top. Top another graham cracker with a marshmallow. Put the plate inside your cooker and let the food cook so the chocolate begins to melt. When your chocolate is melted, stick the two halves together—a s'more! Don't open your cooker too many times, or you will let the warm air out.

The Science Behind the Fun

How does light from the Sun end up as heat to cook food? First, sunlight enters the clear top of your cooker. The light hits the black paper at the bottom, and the black paper gives off heat that heats up the air inside the box. The plastic top and the rolled-up newspaper keep the hot air from escaping, and the temperature inside can heat up to 125°F (about 50°C) or even more. While it is true that solar cookers take a LONG while to heat up and cook food, they use completely free energy!

If you try other foods in your cooker, *don't use foods with raw eggs, mayonnaise, or raw meat.* Your cooker may not get hot enough to kill all the bad bacteria. Use meats that are already cooked, or vegetables or fruits. Try making baked peach slices with cinnamon and honey, baked hot dog pieces, or kale chips!

Solar ovens may be a great idea for areas of the world with no electricity. NASA also uses solar energy in a lot of ways, but especially to make electricity to power spacecraft and the International Space Station.

Fig. 2: Tape black paper inside the box.

Fig. 3: Put newspaper rolls inside the box.

Fig. 4: Shine sunlight into your cooker.

Glowing Water

Time

5 minutes

Materials

- 2 clear drinking glasses
- Tonic water
- Tap water
- Your science notebook
- Pencil

Safety Tips and Setup Hints

- This lab only works if you use tonic water that has quinine (pronounced KWY-nine) in it. Look for "contains quinine" or "tonic water with quinine" on the label. It is the quinine that causes the effect we will see.

- Do this lab on a sunny day, especially around the time when the Sun is highest in the sky.

A special kind of water can glow and show you what your eyes normally can't see.

Instructions

Step 1: Pour tonic water into one glass so it is mostly full. Pour tap water into the other glass so it is mostly full. Observe the tonic water and the tap water while you have them inside the house. See anything interesting? (Fig. 1)

Step 2: Take the full glasses and the black paper or plastic outside in the sunlight, and set up the glasses on a table or something sturdy. Make sure you know which glass has which water. (Fig. 2)

Step 3: Look at the surfaces of the tap water and tonic water as they sit out in the sunlight. What do you see now? (Fig. 3)

Step 4: Try this lab at different times of day. What do you notice when you do it around 8 or 9 a.m., around noon or 1 p.m., and around 3 or 4 p.m.? Try this lab at different times of year. What do you notice when you do it in the winter versus the summer? Write your observations in your notebook to compare. ✦

Fig. 1: Pour tonic water into one glass and tap water into the other glass.

Fig. 2: Set up your tonic and tap waters outside.

Creative Enrichment

You can detect UV light with more than just tonic water. Look for UV-sensitive (or "Sun sensitive") beads, flying discs, paper, wristbands, or clothing. These materials change colors when they are exposed to UV light. There are many experiments you can do with these materials. Take them out at different times of day to see how the color is affected. Take them out when it is sunny, partly cloudy, and completely cloudy to see if there is still enough UV light to make them change color. Try smearing different sunscreens on them and leave them out to see what happens. Test different sunglasses for UV protection. See if different clothes or materials might provide some UV protection. Take pictures during your experiments so you can compare the colors later. Use your imagination to come up with more ideas. The sky is the limit!

Fig. 3: See the water glowing?

The Science Behind the Fun

Our Sun gives off lots of different kinds of energy. The energy our eyes can detect is called "visible light." In this lab, we used tonic water to detect another type of light our eyes can't see, called "ultraviolet light." "Ultra" in "ultraviolet" means "beyond," so the word *ultraviolet* means "beyond the violet" or beyond the violet color of light in the rainbow.

You may have heard of ultraviolet, or UV, light. There are three groups of UV light, based on how much energy the UV light has. UVA light, which is the lowest-energy UV light, is given off by black lightbulbs. We can see a little of the visible light from black lights as a purple color, but much of the light from the bulb is UVA light our eyes can't see. Some paints react to UVA light by turning bright colors. Our skin reacts to UVA light from the Sun by tanning. UVB light has more energy than UVA light, and it is UVB light that gives us a sunburn. You can get a sunburn even when it is cloudy because UVB light can pass through clouds. You can also get nasty sunburns when you are on snow or at the beach because snow and sand reflect UVB light. There is a third type of UV light, called "UVC." It has even more energy than UVB light, but none of the UVC light reaches the ground because of a special layer in our atmosphere: the ozone layer.

The ozone layer is about 15 miles (25 km) above the Earth's surface. The ozone layer does not block UVA light, it blocks most UVB light, and it blocks all UVC light. Without an ozone layer, all the Sun's UV light would hit the ground, and this would be very, very bad for life on Earth.

"Measuring" the Speed of Light

Time

5 minutes

Materials

- Microwave oven
- 2 sturdy dinner-size paper plates
- Plain chocolate bar
- Ruler or tape measure
- Calculator that can display at least 11 digits at once

Safety Tips and Setup Hints

- Do not use a regular plate for this lab. It will absorb energy and give you incorrect results.
- If your microwave oven contains a turntable to rotate food, remove the turntable plate. The turntable allows food to cook evenly, and you want the chocolate to cook unevenly for this lab to work best.
- Be careful when handling chocolate that has been melted in the microwave. It may be very hot and could cause burns if touched, and, if it is in the microwave for too long, it will begin to burn.

Calculating the speed of light is as easy as pie? No. It's as easy as melting chocolate!

Fig. 1: Two plates and a chocolate bar

Instructions

Step 1: Remove the glass turntable from your microwave. Place one paper plate upside down on the floor of the microwave. Place the second paper plate right side up on top of the first plate. The bottoms of both plates should touch each other. Place the chocolate bar on the top plate. If your bar has a flat side, place it flat side up. (Fig. 1)

Step 2: Microwave the chocolate bar at full power for twenty-five to fifty seconds, or until you start to see melted chocolate spots.

Step 3: Measure the distance between the "hot spots" of melted chocolate using your ruler. You can use inches or centimeters. Work quickly! The spot of melted chocolate may spread, making your measurement more difficult or less accurate. (Fig. 2)

Step 4: Multiply this measured distance by two. Then, multiply that calculated number by 2,450,000,000. This will be your calculation for the speed of light, often abbreviated as "c." If you measured the chocolate hot spot distance in inches, your "c" will be in inches per second; if you measured the hot spot distance in centimeters, your "c" will be in centimeters per second. (Fig. 3)

Fig. 2: Measure the distance between the melted hot spots.

The Science Behind the Fun

"Visible light," the type of light our eyes can see, travels at a constant speed, called the "speed of light." Microwaves are another form of light and also travel at this same speed. While our eyes cannot see microwave energy, we can see the "imprint" of these microwaves as melted chocolate hot spots.

Wavelength is how scientists tell different kinds of energy apart. Radio waves have the longest wavelengths, and gamma rays have extremely short wavelengths. The distance between the melted spots measures half a wavelength of the microwaves emitted by your oven. We first multiplied the **hot spot distance** by **2** to determine the span of a whole wavelength.

The speed of light is calculated as *wavelength multiplied by frequency*. The number 2,450,000,000 is the frequency of most modern microwaves: 2,450,000,000 waves that pass by a given point in a second. Therefore, **your wavelength in inches or centimeters** multiplied by **2,450,000,000 waves per second** gives you **the speed of light in inches or centimeters per second.**

The speed of light in air is 11,799,312,883 inches per second, or 29,970,254,724 centimeters per second. So, how close were you? Your result might be off by a bit, but this is absolutely to be expected. There is uncertainty in your hot spot measurement because the hot spots are extended areas, not single points—but if you got anywhere close to the right answer, you did a great job!

Creative Enrichment

Do you get easier-to-measure hot spots if you use chocolate chips? How about using regular-size chips versus miniature chips? White chocolate? Dark chocolate? A plate full of chocolate sprinkles, mini marshmallows, or whipped egg whites? What do these changes do to your calculated results?

Fig. 3: Calculate the speed of light.

Exploring Our Solar System

Many people ask, "Who discovered the planets?" Well, people have always known about Mercury, Venus, Mars, Jupiter, and Saturn. They kind of look like stars, but they don't move in the sky exactly like the stars do, and ancient people noticed this. Greek people from long ago called these objects "planetes." The word *planetes* meant "wanderers." The planetes appeared to wander around the sky. What does the word *planetes* remind you of? Of course—planets! That is where the English word *planet* comes from.

Now, ancient people did not know what planets were. We started to know a lot more about them when we could look at them with telescopes. When Galileo and others looked at them with their telescopes, they could see that they weren't points of light. Telescopes showed they were round, and as our telescopes got better and better, they could see light and dark areas on Mars, stripes on Jupiter, and a ring around Saturn. People used telescopes to find Uranus, Neptune, Pluto, asteroids, and lots of comets. Then, instead of just counting things and seeing how they move, we wanted to know what they were like and how things work there.

In this next set of activities, you'll learn why some things in our Solar System look the way they do, compare some places to others, and find out why Mars really isn't red. You'll get to know our Solar System in fun ways!

As Saturn goes around the Sun, its tilt lets us see different parts at different times. This tilt also makes seasons on Saturn.

Credit: NASA and The Hubble Heritage Team (STScI/AURA)

Sorting Our Solar System

Time
15 minutes

Materials
- At least 30 pictures of objects or places in our Solar System (the more pictures, the better!)
- Several pieces of paper
- Pencil, pen, or marker

Safety Tips and Setup Hints
- NASA has lots of pictures of objects in our Solar System. Use a mix of close-up and faraway images. You can see and print them from:
  - **Planets and dwarf planets:** photojournal.jpl.nasa.gov
  - **Solar System objects:** hubblesite.org/gallery/album/ solar_system
  - **Comets and asteroids:** photojournal.jpl.nasa.gov/ target/Other
- You can also cut out pictures of planets, moons, asteroids, and comets from astronomy and science magazines. See if your local library is having a used book or magazine sale, or contact a local astronomy club to ask if they have copies of astronomy magazines a member wants to give away.

Scientists put things in groups all the time. Try your hand at sorting our Solar System.

Instructions

Step 1: Lay out the pictures so you can see them all. (Fig. 1)

Step 2: One person will sort the pictures into two or more groups of his or her own choice. Be creative! You do not have to choose groups like "planets," "moons," "asteroids," or "comets." Choose groups based on colors, shapes, whether the objects contain craters (or not), objects that are close to the Sun, objects that are far from the Sun, rocky things, icy things, things with stripes, round things versus things that aren't round, or anything else you would like to choose. There are no right answers, and you do not have to use all the pictures. Make labels for each group, but do not show the labels to the other person yet. (Fig. 2)

Step 3: A second person will try to figure out the groups chosen by the first person. Did you figure out the groups correctly?

Step 4: Switch roles. The second person should now try to make new groups, and the first person should try to figure out what they are. Do this as many times as you want!

Fig. 1: Display your pictures.

Creative Enrichment

When you are done with this lab, make an art collage of as many pretty Solar System pictures as you can find. Use real pictures for some of your images. Try making sketches of some images using interesting colors. Use other materials to add to some of the pictures, such as glitter, construction paper, tissue paper, ribbon, or natural things, such as leaves, dried flowers, twigs, or grasses. Group your pictures any way you want!

The Science Behind the Fun

Did you notice when you did this lab you could put the same picture into different groups? Scientists like to group things, too. In our Solar System, we have one star: our Sun. There are eight planets: Mercury, Venus, Earth, Mars, Jupiter, Saturn, Uranus, and Neptune, and we know of at least 173 moons. We can make many groups of planets, such as "planets with rings" and "planets with no rings," or "large planets" and "small planets," or "planets with moons" and "planets without moons." There are many thousands of comets, which are city-size chunks of ice and rock. There are more than two hundred thousand asteroids that are a few tens of feet (a few meters) across to the largest asteroid, which is 590 miles (950 km) across. Even asteroids can be grouped, such as "asteroids that pass close to Earth," "asteroids between Mars and Jupiter," and others.

There are at least five dwarf planets in our Solar System, which means that these objects are round and they orbit the Sun. One of the dwarf planets is Ceres (pronounced SEER-reez), which is also an asteroid. But wait—how can something be an asteroid AND a dwarf planet? How can something be in more than one group? You probably put the same picture in more than one group, and this happens in science all the time. Both groups are correct!

Fig. 2: Sort your pictures into groups.

How to "See" a Surface When You Can't See a Surface

Time

1 hour

Materials

- Plastic straw
- Ruler or tape measure with centimeter marks
- Permanent marker
- 1 cardboard box with a separate lid, such as a shoe box
- Pencil
- Scissors (or something sharp to poke holes in the box lid)
- A set of plastic snap-together bricks
- Your science notebook

Safety Tips and Setup Hints

- An adult should be the one to make the holes in the box lid.

There are some places in the Solar System we can't see easily. So, how do we see them?

Instructions

Step 1: Lay the straw on a table and put the zero end of your ruler at one end of the straw. Using the permanent marker, put a small mark on the straw every centimeter along its whole length. Don't let the straw roll! Label each centimeter (1, 2, 3, and so on) along the straw. (Fig. 1)

Step 2: Lay your box lid on the table and put the zero end of your ruler at one of the short edges of the lid. Using the pencil, put a small mark along the long edge of the lid every two centimeters. Do the same thing along the other long edge (and make sure your marks line up).

Then, put the zero end of your ruler at one of the long edges of the lid. Using the pencil, put a small mark along the short edge of the lid every two centimeters. Do the same thing along the other short edge.

Finally, line up the marks with the ruler along opposite edges and draw a line with the pencil to connect the dots in a straight line. Do this for all the marks along the long edges of the box and along the short edges of the box. You should end up with a set of squares all over the top of the box. (Why use pencil? If your marks aren't in the right place, you can erase them and remeasure.) (Fig. 2)

Step 3: Where your grid lines come together, have an adult make a hole using scissors or the pointy end of a sharp knife. You should end up with a grid of holes all over the top of your box. Make sure the holes are big enough for your straw to go through easily. (Fig. 3)

Fig. 1: Turn your straw into a ruler.

Fig. 2: Draw a grid on your box lid.

Fig. 3: Poke holes in the top of the box.

Step 4: Have someone else make a "planet surface" inside the box so you don't see it. Have that person snap different bricks together and make a surface with different heights all over the inside of the box. Don't peek! Your partner should put the lid on the box without showing the inside to you. (Fig. 4)

Step 5: In your science notebook, draw a grid that matches your lid. If your lid is six holes wide and fifteen holes long, draw the same grid in your science notebook. Starting at one end of the box, put the zero end of the straw through the first hole in the box. Push the straw in until it hits something and stops. Look at your straw and record the measurement in your notebook. If the straw ends up between marks, record the number of the first mark you can see above the hole. Do the same for all the holes, and record measurements for every hole in your notebook. (Fig. 5)

Step 6: Look at your notebook. Can you tell which parts of the surface in the box are taller and which parts are shorter? Lift the lid to see if you are right! ◆

Fig. 4: Make a bumpy planet surface inside the box.

Fig. 5: Measure the inside of the box using the straw.

The Science Behind the Fun

There are places in our Solar System where we can't easily see what's there. How do we "see" these surfaces, then? The answer is RADAR. "RADAR" stands for "RAdio Detection and Ranging." A radar system uses radio waves pointed toward a surface. The radio waves travel at the speed of light, hit the surface, and travel back to the system. Radar systems can tell us things, such as how high a surface is, what temperature it is, or what the surface looks like. NASA's *Cassini* spacecraft used radar to study the hazy surface of Saturn's moon Titan, and NASA's *Magellan* spacecraft used radar to study the cloud-covered surface of Venus. In our lab, we couldn't send out radio or sound waves, so we used the straw as our way to figure out where the top of the surface was inside the box. You can change the surface inside the box as often as you like! Challenge your friends or family to the same lab. How did they do?

Creative Enrichment

Look at your measurements of the surface inside the box. How would you show higher parts of the surface on a flat piece of paper? How would you show lower parts? Try to draw a map just by using your grid and those measurements.

Hole-y Surfaces!

Time
15 to 20 minutes

Materials

- 1 pan about 8 to 12 inches (20 to 30 cm) long and about 4 inches (10 cm) deep
- Newspaper or plastic sheeting
- Enough flour to fill your pan about three-fourths full (the amount will depend on the size of your pan)
- 1 or 2 small bottles of colored sugar
- About ½ to 1 cup (43 to 86 g) of cocoa powder
- Flour sifter or small fine-mesh strainer
- A handful of small rocks or marbles of various sizes (no more than 2 inches [5 cm] in diameter)
- Ruler or tape measure

Safety Tips and Setup Hints

- Do not substitute hot chocolate mix for the cocoa powder. There is not enough color contrast between the mix and the flour to make the cratering effects stand out.
- For easy cleanup, do this lab outside or put newspaper or plastic sheeting under your pan.

Let's see how craters are made and how we can learn about surfaces by studying them.

Instructions

Step 1: Fill your pan about halfway full of flour. Then, shake a layer of colored sugar over the surface of the flour, covering the flour completely with the colored sugar. (Fig. 1)

Step 2: With the sifter, sift a layer of flour over the sugared layer, filling your pan about three-fourths of the way total. Next, sift a layer of cocoa powder over the flour, covering the flour completely. You should end up with a pan with several layers; from the bottom up, your pan will contain flour, then colored sugar above, then flour, and finally cocoa powder on the top. (Fig. 2)

Step 3: Drop a rock into the flour. You can see the different layers represented by the different colors of materials. What happened? Which material went farthest? Which material didn't travel quite as far? (Fig. 3)

Step 4: Try dropping rocks of different sizes from the same height, measuring the height using your ruler or tape measure. What differences do you see in the craters? Next, drop rocks of the same size from different heights, representing objects traveling at different speeds. How are your craters the same or different? (If your pan is small, you may have to reapply the flour, sugar, and cocoa powder layers periodically.) ◆

Fig. 1: Sprinkle colored sugar on your flour.

Fig. 2: You are ready to create some craters!

The Science Behind the Fun

A crater can form when an object from space smashes into the surface of a world. The hole is usually roughly circular in shape. The size of the resulting crater depends on many different factors, such as the speed, density, size, or angle of the impacting object, and the density of the surface that is struck. (Fig. 4)

Scientists are very interested in studying craters because they not only can tell you about the impact event itself, but this natural process has also excavated a way for you to see into a surface without having to dig the hole yourself! There are about 175 known impact craters on Earth and untold millions on many other worlds. Why don't we see many craters on Earth? Earth's surface is very geologically active, and the rocky surface is continually changing due to plate tectonics, volcanoes, and the weathering action of wind and water. Friction with Earth's atmosphere causes many smaller objects to burn up before reaching the surface, so only larger objects strike and create craters. In addition, 70 percent of Earth's surface is covered by water, meaning quite a few objects that are able to survive to the surface fall harmlessly into the ocean.

Creative Enrichment

You can try different types of materials in your cratering pan, representing different surfaces found in our Solar System:

Earth: Use the same flour/sugar/flour/cocoa powder surface, but after you make a few craters, use a mister or hand sprayer bottle to spray your craters lightly with water, representing weathering over time. What happens to your craters after five sprays as water interacts with them? Ten sprays? More sprays?

Wet Mars: Mix dirt and water to make mud, though don't make it soupy. This represents some of the Martian surfaces we have seen that seem to indicate that craters occurred on Mars when liquid water was just under the surface a long time ago. Make your craters using this surface. How do these craters differ from the others?

Frozen Mars: Freeze a thin layer of water in your pan for an hour or two, and then cover it with a layer of fine sand. This represents ice just below the Martian surface, something we have seen on Mars recently. You may have to throw your impactor vigorously to go through the ice layer. How are these frozen Mars craters different from the wet Mars craters?

Fig. 4: This is a 100-foot-diameter (30 m) crater on the surface of Mars, the result of an impact that occurred sometime between July 2010 and May 2012. Material was thrown as far as nine miles (15 km) away.

Fig. 3: A very hole-y surface!

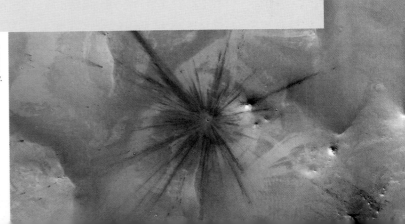

Is the Red Planet Actually Red?

Time
3 to 7 days

Materials
- 1 or 2 steel wool pads
- Sharp scissors
- 2 small containers of sand or small pebbles
- Spray bottle filled with water
- Plastic wrap

Safety Tips and Setup Hints
- Have an adult cut up the steel wool into small pieces using sharp scissors. Be careful. The steel wool pieces can be sharp. Use heavy work gloves when handling them, and do not rub your eyes or skin after handling the steel wool. Wash your hands when you are done.

We call Mars the "Red Planet." Is it?

Instructions

Step 1: Carefully mix the steel wool pieces with the sand or pebbles in one container. Do not do anything to the sand in the other container. (Fig. 1)

Step 2: Spray the top of the sand or pebbles in both containers lightly with the water five to seven times. (Fig. 2)

Step 3: Cover the containers with plastic wrap. (Fig. 3)

Step 4: Every day, spray the sand in both containers again and cover the containers again. After a few days, compare the sand or pebbles in both containers. Are there any differences? (Fig. 4) ✦

This feature on Mars is called Ma'adim Valles. *Ma'adim* is the Hebrew word for the planet Mars. Ma'adim Valles is likely a dried river that flowed north to the crater at the top of the picture, called Gusev (GOO-sev) Crater. Gusev Crater is where NASA's *Spirit* rover landed in January 2004. This picture of Ma'adim Valles was taken by one of NASA's *Viking* orbiters in the 1970s.

Credit: NASA/JPL–Caltech

The Science Behind the Fun

When you think of the color red, what do you think of? Maybe you think of stop signs, apples, or exit signs. Have you seen pictures of Mars? Is Mars the same red color as those other red things? Not exactly. Mars may be called the Red Planet, but it really isn't bright red at all. Parts of Mars can be reddish brown and other parts are gray. These reddish and gray minerals on Mars are really just the same mineral, called "hematite" (pronounced HE-muh-tite). The red version of this mineral is the same as the gray version; the red version is just the gray version ground up into a smaller powder, causing it to look red. The rust you made in your bowl is a cousin to the hematite we have found on Mars.

Was Mars wet in the distant past? Yes it was! Scientists have seen many signs of long ago liquid water on Mars, including evidence of gullies, streams, hot springs, and dried riverbeds.

Creative Enrichment

Would you like to see places on Earth similar to Mars? Do a search online for pictures of these locations:

- Ubehebe Crater and Mars Hill, both in Death Valley National Park, California
- Mono Lake, California
- Channeled Scablands in Washington
- Volcanoes in Hawai'i Volcanoes National Park

Make a travel brochure for one of these spots. Find out where it is, how to get there, how to explore there safely, and how your chosen spot is like Mars. For even more fun, use your travel brochure to plan and lead a family trip! It's like going to Mars—only easier!

Fig. 1: Mix in the steel wool.

Fig. 2: Spray both containers with water.

Fig. 3: Cover both containers.

Fig. 4: What does the sand look like after a few days?

Time

A few hours to a few days

Materials

- 3 glass Mason jars with lids
- 9 cups (3.15 L) of sand or tiny pebbles
- 4 teaspoons (24 g) of salt
- 4 teaspoons (18 g) of baking powder
- 2 packets of dry yeast (1 packet of yeast is about 2 teaspoons, or 9 g)
- 1 large pitcher
- 1 cup (200 g) of sugar
- 3 cups (710 ml) of warm water (100° to 110°F, or 37° to 43°C)
- Cookie sheet
- Your science notebook
- Pencil

Safety Tips and Setup Hints

- You will do this experiment twice. Pay attention to the amounts in the instructions.
- Label each jar so you can tell them apart later. The first jar should be labeled "salt," the second jar should be labeled "baking powder," and the third jar should be labeled "yeast."

The *Viking* spacecraft looked for signs of life on Mars in the 1970s. What did they find?

Instructions

Step 1: Fill each jar with 1½ cups (350 g) of sand. Pour 2 teaspoons of salt into the first jar. Pour 2 teaspoons of baking powder into the second jar. Pour one packet of yeast into the third jar. Put the lids on each jar.

Step 2: *Gently* shake the jars to mix the ingredients into the sand. Remove the lids. (Fig. 1)

Step 3: Pour ½ cup (100 g) of sugar into 1½ cups (about 300 ml) of warm water. Stir the water with a spoon until the sugar is dissolved. You'll know it is dissolved when you don't feel the crunchy sugar crystals when you stir the water, and the water will look clear again.

Step 4: Pour about ½ cup (about 120 ml) of sugar water into each jar. Put the jars onto the cookie sheet to prevent spills. (Fig. 2)

Step 5: Observe what happens in each jar, checking back every hour or so. Record the results in your science notebook. Let the jars sit overnight, and observe them the next day. What did you notice?

Step 6: Pour all the sand out of each jar (ask an adult where to put the sand). Clean each jar. Repeat the experiment by putting sand into each jar, and adding the salt, baking powder, and yeast into the jars. Use the same amounts as described in step 1. Put the lids on the jars, and gently shake the jars. Take the lids off the jars. This time, put all three jars into the freezer, and let them sit overnight or, even better, for a few days. Take the jars out of the freezer, and repeat the experiment by adding the warm sugar water to each jar. Observe what happens. What do you notice this time? ◆

Creative Enrichment

You can use yeast in other ways—such as making bread! There is a type of bread called "Amish Friendship Bread" that starts with flour, milk, sugar, and yeast. The sugar feeds the yeast, and the yeast gives off gas. Every few days more milk and flour are added, and sugar is added so the yeast has even more food to eat. After a few more days, the batter is ready to use, and some of it can be given away to friends so they can make their own friendship bread. Give it a try!

Fig. 1: Prepare your jars.

The Science Behind the Fun

In 1976 NASA landed two spacecraft on Mars, called *Viking 1* and *Viking 2*. One of the questions scientists hoped to answer was whether there was life on the surface of Mars. This would not be life like people or animals, but smaller life, such as bacteria. When chemicals are added to soil containing bacteria that can eat the chemicals as food, then the sample would give off gas as long as there is food to feed the bacteria. If there were no bacteria, then only a little gas or no gas at all would be released. What did NASA find out? There were mixed results. One experiment showed a release of gas, like you would see if life was there, but two other experiments didn't show any signs of life. Experiments on future Mars landers may help answer the question of whether there was, or is, life on Mars.

In this experiment, the sand represents Mars soil. The salt and baking powder represent different chemicals in Mars soil. The yeast represents bacteria. When the warm sugar water was added to the first set of sand in the jars, the yeast ate the sugar and gave off lots of gas for a while, until they ate all the sugar. In the second experiment, the jars were put into the freezer to represent the cold surface of Mars.

Fig. 2: Pour in the sugar water.

YEAST

Cool Crystals

Time

A few hours to overnight

Materials

- For Epsom salt crystals:
  - Small, deep bowl
  - ½ cup (120 ml) hot water from the faucet
  - ½ cup (120 g) Epsom salt
  - Food coloring (any color)
- For table salt crystals:
  - Small pot
  - 1 cup (240 ml) distilled water
  - Noniodized salt (amount will vary)
  - Piece of cardboard small enough to fit into the pot
  - Plate
- For the borax crystals:
  - Up to 4 cups (950 ml) of water
  - 1 Mason jar
  - Up to 1 cup (240 ml) of borax
  - Food coloring (any color)
  - Pipe cleaner (also called a "chenille stem")
  - 3 inches (7.5 cm) of string
  - Straw or pencil

(Continues on page 58)

You can make several kinds of crystals using everyday things.

Instructions

Step 1: For the Epsom salt crystals, pour the hot water into the bowl, add a few drops of food coloring, and stir in the Epsom salt until most of it dissolves. Some crunchy bits will still be at the bottom of the bowl. Put the bowl in the refrigerator. After a few days, check the bowl. What do you see? (Fig. 1)

Step 2: For the table salt crystals, boil the water in a small pot on the stove. Slowly stir salt into the boiling water until no more salt will dissolve. You will know enough is added when salt pieces stay on the bottom of the pot and the bottom of the pot will feel a little crunchy. Turn off the stove. (Fig. 2)

Step 3: Have an adult carefully soak a small piece of cardboard in the hot salty water. When it is soggy, put it on a plate, and put it in a warm spot in the sunlight outside. Watch it for a few hours as it dries out. What do you see? (Fig. 3)

Step 4: For the borax crystals, boil the water and carefully pour it into the jar. Stir in the borax until no more can dissolve. A few crunchy bits will be on the bottom of the jar. Put a few drops of food coloring into the jar. (Fig. 4)

(Continues on page 58)

Fig. 1: Make Epsom salt crystals.

Safety Tips and Setup Hints

(Continued from page 56)

- Make sure an adult helps with making these crystals, especially the parts using hot or boiling water. Be careful!

- Do not eat the Epsom salt crystals or the borax crystals. **They are not edible.** The salt crystals contain a lot of salt, so it is best not to eat them.

- For the table salt crystals, use salt that does not have iodine in it. It will be called "noniodized" salt.

- Epsom salt is available in the first-aid section of a drugstore and many grocery stores. Powdered borax is available in the laundry detergent section of a grocery store.

Step 5: Twist one end of the pipe cleaner into whatever shape you want. The shape should be able to fit into the jar. Tie a piece of string to the pipe cleaner handle. Tie the other end of the string to the straw or pencil so the pipe cleaner can hang into the jar without touching the bottom of the jar. Put the pipe cleaner into the borax water in the jar. Let the jar sit for a few days. Don't move it or touch it. What do you see?

Fig. 2: Make table salt crystals.

The Science Behind the Fun

If you live in a place where there is snow, catch a few snowflakes and look at them up close. Snowflakes are crystals, too! A crystal is a hard material made of bits that come together in patterns to form interesting shapes. Salt crystals usually form cube shapes, Epsom salt crystals form needle shapes, and other materials form different shapes.

Minerals also come in crystal shapes. These mineral crystals can tell us a lot. Some of the oldest known bits of Earth's crust are crystals called "zircon." Some types of meteorites contain different kinds of crystals, and we can learn about what the early Solar System was like from meteorites. Rovers on Mars have found crystals of gypsum (pronounced JIP-sum), which tells us that some parts of Mars had hot water springs. When the hot water dried, the gypsum crystals were left behind in the rock. We can learn about lots of surfaces in our Solar System by studying minerals and crystals!

Creative Enrichment

There are lots of recipes for making sugar crystals, also called "rock sugar candy." Look up a recipe online or in a kitchen science experiment book, and have an adult help you make it. Also, if you need something else to do with your box of borax after you make borax crystals, check out recipes online for making different types of slime. You can't eat the slime, but it is fun to make it!

Fig. 4: Make the borax water.

Fig. 3: Soak the cardboard in the salt water.

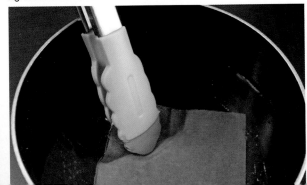

ORION.

Taurus.

Gemini.

Monoceros.

Cetus.

Æquator.

Æquator.

Eridanus.

Fig. QQ.

Canis Major.

Lepus.

Seeing Stars

People have always looked up at the stars and wondered about them. Stars have been used by adults to teach important lessons to children. Knowing the sky and the ocean allowed very skilled people to travel over the Pacific Ocean thousands of years before GPS. People were connected to the sky, and the stars were a part of everyone's everyday life. Different people around the world were connected to the stars in different ways.

In 1922, astronomers separated the entire sky into eighty-eight constellations, like drawing borders on a map. Each star is a part of only one constellation. The reason they did this was to help scientists tell one another where in the sky they studied different things so all the scientists were using the same set of maps.

Go outside to try to find different groups of stars. It might seem very confusing at first, but if you start with certain stars, such as the Big Dipper or Orion's belt, you can find many others. Give it a try and get to know the sky!

This is a drawing of the constellation Orion the Hunter from the year 1690. This picture shows Orion a little differently from how we see Orion in the real sky. How is it different? Try Lab 49, "Find the Hunter in the Winter" (see page 132), and find out!

Credit: Johannes Hevelius

Find the Dipper and the Pole in Spring

Time

10 minutes

✂ Materials

- Your science notebook
- Pencil

Safety Tips and Setup Hints

- Be careful when you are out-side looking at the sky. Make sure you are in a safe location. Wear reflective or light-colored clothing so people can see you.

- If you go out of town to a dark location, have an adult call the nonemergency phone number of the local police to let them know where you are and what you will be doing. Do not set up on private property without the property owner's permis-sion. Follow all local laws. Beware that in many towns, parks close at sunset.

- If you are outside for a long time, you can get cold, even when it isn't that cold. Dress in comfortable layers.

- These instructions work best in May.

To learn your way around the sky, begin with the Big Dipper.

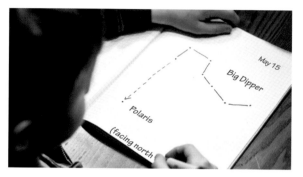

Fig. 2: Sketch the Big Dipper and Polaris.

Instructions

Step 1: Go outside about an hour after sunset in May and face north. If you aren't sure which direction is north, then during the daytime, use Lab 3, "Determining Directions" (see page 16), or use a compass.

Step 2: Look up. The Big Dipper will be hanging "upside down" above you. The bowl of the Big Dipper will be on the left, and the crooked handle will be on the right. Once you find it, sketch it in your notebook. (Fig. 1)

Step 3: Continue to face north. Try to spot the Dipper's crooked handle on the right and the four stars that form the bowl of the Dipper on the left. Look for the two stars on the left side of the bowl. Draw a straight line between those two stars and follow the line down. The next star you run into will be Polaris, the North Star. Make a sketch in your notebook if you found Polaris. (Fig. 2) ◆

Creative Enrichment

There are lots of star maps and constellation books available. If you have a smartphone, get an app that shows you what is in the night sky. Use these resources to plan a family star party! Bring activities for family members to do, make sure everyone dresses in the right clothing, bring bug spray and your science notebook, and don't forget hot chocolate and snacks! Go out as often as you can, and you will start to learn how to find your way around the night sky.

Discover what other people call the Big Dipper. For example, in some parts of the world, the same stars are called the Plow or the Wagon. What else do other people see using those same stars?

The Science Behind the Fun

The Big Dipper is one of the easier groups of stars to find. The shape of the Dipper stars looks like a soup pot with a crooked handle. If you go out to find the Big Dipper, don't worry if you can't see it right away. Finding things in the sky takes practice. The Big Dipper is part of a larger constellation called Ursa Major, the Great Bear. The rest of the stars of the Great Bear are dimmer and harder to see.

Did you notice that Polaris is not very bright? That's because it isn't. There are about forty other stars in the sky that are brighter than the North Star. The reason the North Star is important is that our Earth's North Pole points almost directly at it. As the Earth turns, the stars seem to rise in the east and set in the west, and they appear to turn around the North Star. It looks like it stays in one place. About an hour after sunset in the spring, the Big Dipper will be high up in the north. About an hour after sunset in the summer, the Big Dipper will be in the northwest sky with the bowl pointing down. About an hour after sunset in the fall, the Big Dipper will be low in the sky to the north with the bowl to the right, and about an hour after sunset in the winter, the Big Dipper will be in the northeast sky standing on its handle.

Where you live may change your sky. If you live farther south, things in the sky to the north will be lower. If you live farther north, things in the sky to the north will be higher.

Fig. 1: Look for the Big Dipper in the northern sky.

Time

10 minutes

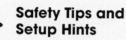

Materials

- Your science notebook
- Pencil

Safety Tips and Setup Hints

- Be careful when you are outside looking at the sky. Make sure you are in a safe location. Wear reflective or light-colored clothing so people can see you.

- If you go out of town to a dark location, have an adult call the nonemergency phone number of the local police to let them know where you are and what you will be doing. Do not set up on private property without the property owner's permission. Follow all local laws. Beware that in many towns, parks close at sunset.

- If you are outside for a long time, you can get cold, even when it isn't that cold. Dress in comfortable layers.

- These instructions work best in September.

Three bright stars form a big triangle in the warm summer sky.

Instructions

Step 1: Go outside about two hours after sunset and face south. If you aren't sure which direction is south, then during the daytime, use Lab 3, "Determining Directions" (see page 16), or use a compass. (Fig. 1)

Step 2: Look overhead or nearly overhead. Try to find three bright stars that form a large triangle in the sky. Once you find it, sketch it in your notebook. (Fig. 2)

Step 3: To test your sky skills, try finding the Big Dipper stars from Lab 46, "Find the Dipper and the Pole in Spring" (see page 62). Face north. The Big Dipper will be toward the northwest, or to the left of north. Do you see them? The bowl stars will be on the bottom and the handle will be pointing up.

Step 4: To find another star, look toward the northwest sky and find the Big Dipper. Notice the handle is curved, like part of a circle. Follow the curve away from the bowl toward the south until you see another really bright star. It will have a little bit of an orange color. This is the star called Arcturus (ark-TUR-rus). Make another sketch in your notebook if you can find it. (Fig. 3)

Fig. 1: Go out and look up.

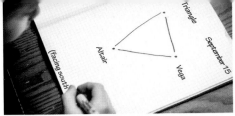

Fig. 2: Sketch the three triangle stars.

Fig. 3: Follow the arc to Arcturus.

The Science Behind the Fun

As the Earth goes around the Sun, we see different stars depending on the season. The summer sky has lots of bright stars. Face south again. The star in the triangle that is farthest south is called Altair (ALL-tare). The other two stars form the other sides of the triangle, and they are a little farther north than Altair. The one that is on the right, or west, is called Vega (VAY-guh). The star to the left, or east, is called Deneb (DEN-neb). The triangle is made of three stars that are part of three different constellations. Altair is the brightest star in the constellation called Aquila (uh-KWIL-luh) the Eagle. Vega is the brightest star in a small constellation called Lyra (LIE-ruh) the Harp. Deneb is the brightest star in the constellation called Cygnus (SIG-nus) the Swan. The other stars that form those constellations are dimmer, so they can be harder to find, but the triangle can be easier to find since those three stars are bright. This triangle is called the Summer Triangle because it is high in the sky in the summer and early fall after sunset.

A constellation is a group of stars that forms a picture of something, like a connect-the-dots picture. Did you try to find stars that might have looked like a small harp? It's really hard to do, right? If you don't see a harp, or an eagle, or a swan, don't worry. That's because many of the constellations *don't* look much like what they are named for! Lots of people have trouble seeing them. It is much easier to make your own connect-the-dot pictures—which is okay to do!

Creative Enrichment

The star name Arcturus comes from an old Greek word, *arktos* (ARK-tohs), which means "bear." The Greek name for Arcturus was Arctouros, which meant "bear watcher" or "bear driver" or "bear guard." Think of that star as keeping an eye on the Great or Big Bear (remember, the Big Dipper stars are part of the Big Bear constellation). Our word *arctic* also comes from this same Greek word for bear. Many of the brightest stars in the sky have interesting names. Find out what different people around the world have used as names for Arcturus, Vega, Altair, and Deneb, and find stories about those star names. Draw pictures to represent some of those stories.

LAB 23

Find a Flying Horse in the Fall

Time

10 minutes

Materials

- Your science notebook
- Pencil

Safety Tips and Setup Hints

- Be careful when you are outside looking at the sky. Make sure you are in a safe location. Wear reflective or light-colored clothing so people can see you.

- If you go out of town to a dark location, have an adult call the nonemergency phone number of the local police to let them know where you are and what you will be doing. Do not set up on private property without the property owner's permission. Follow all local laws. Beware that in many towns, parks close at sunset.

- If you are outside for a long time, you can get chilled, even when it isn't that cold. Dress in comfortable layers.

- These instructions work best in November.

Horses aren't shaped like squares, right? Well, in the sky, they are!

Instructions

Step 1: Go outside about three hours after sunset and face south. If you aren't sure which direction is south, then during the daytime, use Lab 3, "Determining Directions" (see page 16), or use a compass. (Fig. 1)

Step 2: Look about halfway up in the sky. Try to find four stars in the shape of a large square. Once you find the square, sketch it in your notebook. (Fig. 2)

Step 3: To test your sky skills, try finding the Summer Triangle stars from Lab 47, "Find the Triangle in the Summer" (see page 64). Face west. The three bright stars will be about halfway up in the sky. The one that is highest is Deneb, and Altair and Vega will be below it. Vega will be to the right and Altair will be to the left. (Fig. 3)

Step 4: Now, face north and look for the Big Dipper stars from Lab 46, "Find the Dipper and the Pole in Spring" (see page 62). The Big Dipper will be very low in the sky near the horizon. The bowl will be to the right and the handle will be to the left. Do you see it? (If you live farther south, the Dipper may be below the horizon and not visible.)

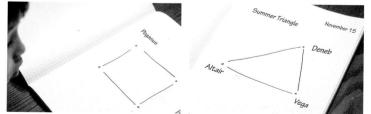

Fig. 2: Sketch the square of stars.

Fig. 3: Sketch the triangle and label the stars.

Creative Enrichment

Put on a play to tell the story of Pegasus, Andromeda, and the others. Use props and costumes. Show your play to your family—and get them to join in if you can!

Fig. 1: Go outside and face south.

The Science Behind the Fun

What is this square of stars in the sky? Would you believe it's a flying horse with wings? This is Pegasus (PEG-guh-sus). Some drawings show the square as the body of Pegasus, while others show the square as the horse's wings. There is no wrong way to draw it, though.

There is a story that uses many of the constellations in the sky that you can see in the fall: *Once upon a time*, there was a beautiful girl named Andromeda (an-DRAH-me-duh). Her father was King Cepheus (SEE-fee-us). Her mother was Queen Cassiopeia (cas-see-o-PEH-uh). One day, Queen Cassiopeia was looking at herself in a mirror when she said, aloud, that she was the most beautiful woman in the world. Well, the guardians of the rivers, streams, and seas, called sea nymphs (pronounced NIMFS), heard her. Since *they* thought *they* were the most beautiful women, they got mad and went to Neptune (NEP-toon), the god of the sea. The nymphs asked Neptune to punish Cassiopeia, so Neptune ordered that Princess Andromeda should be chained to a rock by the sea, and she would become lunch for Cetus (SEE-tus) the sea monster. So, Andromeda was chained to a rock. Everyone was at the beach, crying, while they waited for Cetus to arrive. While Cetus swam toward the beach, a little speck appeared in the sky. It got bigger and bigger. It was Perseus (PER-see-us) riding on the back of Pegasus! Cetus came out of the water to grab Andromeda when, all of a sudden, Perseus pulled the head of Medusa (muh-DEW-suh) out of a bag! Cetus saw it and turned instantly to stone! He fell into the water, never to be seen again. Perseus rescued Andromeda, and they all lived *happily ever after*.

Time

10 minutes

Materials

- Your science notebook
- Pencil

Safety Tips and Setup Hints

- Be careful when you are outside looking at the sky. Make sure you are in a safe location. Wear reflective or light-colored clothing so people can see you.

- If you go out of town to a dark location, have an adult call the nonemergency phone number of the local police to let them know where you are and what you will be doing. Do not set up on private property without the property owner's permission. Follow all local laws. Beware that in many towns, parks close at sunset.

- If you are outside for a long time, you can get chilled, even when it isn't that cold. Dress in comfortable layers.

- These instructions work best in February.

A popular hunter is in the winter sky. If you find his belt, you can find the rest of him!

Instructions

Step 1: Go outside about two hours after sunset and face south. If you aren't sure which direction is south, then during the daytime, use Lab 3, "Determining Directions" (see page 16), or use a compass.

Step 2: Look about halfway up in the sky. Try to find three stars in a row. The star on the left will be a little lower than the star on the right. Once you find it, sketch it in your notebook. (Fig. 1)

Step 3: Look for two stars above the three in a row. They will be bright. The one on the left will be a little more orange in color than the one on the right.

Next, look for two stars below the three in a row. The star on the right will be a little more blue than the star on the left. In all, the three stars in a row, the two stars above, and the two stars below will look like a sideways bow tie. Sketch these stars when you find them. (Fig. 2)

Step 4: To test your sky skills, try finding the square of stars from Lab 48, "Finding a Flying Horse in the Fall" (see page 66). Face west. The square will be on its side pretty low in the western sky. It will look like a square sitting on one of its points. (Fig. 3)

Step 5: Now, face north and look for the Big Dipper stars from Lab 46, "Find the Dipper and the Pole in Spring" (see page 62). The Big Dipper will be in the northeast sky, sitting on its handle with the bowl at the top. ◆

Creative Enrichment

While Orion is the name of this constellation in some parts of the world, it isn't called Orion everywhere. Try to find what other cultures have called the stars of Orion, and make a collage of pictures of what you find.

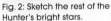

Fig. 1: Sketch the three stars in a row.

Fig. 2: Sketch the rest of the Hunter's bright stars.

The Science Behind the Fun

What is this sideways bow tie of stars? This is Orion (o-RIH-un) the Hunter. Many people have heard of Orion, and the stars are bright. The three stars in a row are Orion's belt. The star up and to the left of the belt is an orange-colored star called Betelgeuse (BAY-tel-joos). The star up and to the right of the belt is called Bellatrix (BELL-uh-tricks). Betelgeuse and Bellatrix are Orion's shoulders. The star below and to the left of the belt is Saiph (SIGH-eef), and the star below and to the right of the belt is a blue-white star called Rigel (RIE-jel).

Lots and lots of people on Earth can see the stars that form Orion. In February, it is winter in the Northern Hemisphere and summer in the Southern Hemisphere. At the North Pole in winter, Orion's belt and shoulders go around the horizon, but his knees are below the horizon and can't be seen. The farther south you go, the higher Orion is in the sky. In the United States, Orion is about halfway up in the winter sky. At the equator, Orion rises in the east, goes directly overhead, and sets in the west. If you keep traveling farther south than the equator, it is summertime. Orion would be lower and lower to the north. If you face north, Orion would be standing on his head!

Fig. 3: Go outside and try to find the square horse.

LAB 25

Slide Around the Winter Sky

Time

10 minutes

✂ Materials

- Your science notebook
- Pencil

⛑ Safety Tips and Setup Hints

- Be careful when you are outside looking at the sky. Make sure you are in a safe location. Wear reflective or light-colored clothing so people can see you.

- If you go out of town to a dark location, have an adult call the nonemergency phone number of the local police to let them know where you are and what you will be doing. Do not set up on private property without the property owner's permission. Follow all local laws. Beware that in many towns, parks close at sunset.

- If you are outside for a long time, you can get chilled, even when it isn't that cold. Dress in comfortable layers.

- These instructions work best in February.

You can use the stars of Orion to find many others.

Instructions

Step 1: Go outside about two hours after sunset and face south. If you aren't sure which direction is south, then during the daytime, use Lab 3, "Determining Directions" (see page 16), or use a compass. (Fig. 1)

Step 2: Look about halfway up in the sky. Try to find the three stars in a row that form Orion the Hunter's belt. The star on the left will be a little lower than the star on the right. Follow Orion's belt up and to the right. Stop when you get to an orange-colored star. This is the star Aldebaran (al-DEB-uh-rahn). Aldebaran will be part of a small V of stars. This V of stars is a cluster, or group, of stars called the Hyades (HIGH-uh-deez). A little to the right of the V is another small group that looks like a really tiny dipper. This tiny group is called the Pleiades (PLEE-uh-deez), or the Seven Sisters. Sketch these stars in your notebook. (Fig. 2)

Step 3: Go back to Orion's belt stars. Follow the belt down and to the left. Stop when you reach a really bright star. This is the star Sirius (SEER-ree-us). Sketch this star in your notebook. (Fig. 3)

Step 4: Look for the two bright stars above Orion's belt. These are Betelgeuse and Bellatrix. Draw a line between Bellatrix and Betelgeuse and follow it to the left. Stop when you get to another bright star. This is the star Procyon (PRO-see-on). If you connect Procyon, Betelgeuse, and Sirius, you should see a triangle, with Procyon and Betelgeuse at the top, and Sirius at the bottom. These three stars are also called the Winter Triangle. Sketch these stars in your notebook. (Fig. 4) ◆

Fig. 1: Go outside and find the Dipper.

Fig. 2: Sketch the small V and the tiny "dipper."

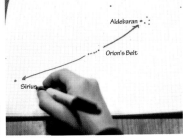

Fig. 3: Sketch Sirius.

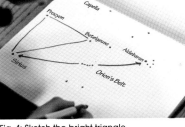

Fig. 4: Sketch the bright triangle.

Creative Enrichment

The Pleiades are often called the Seven Sisters. For centuries, people used the Pleiades to test eyesight. Most people can see four to six stars. Some with really good eyesight can see eight to ten stars. With extremely good eyesight, some people can see thirteen or fourteen stars. Try to see how many you can find when you are out under a really dark sky. Sketch the ones you can see and compare your sketch to a picture of the Pleiades. How did you do? Another eyesight test is the star that is in the bend in the handle of the Big Dipper. This is the star Mizar (MY-zahr). There is a dim star really close to it. This star's name is Alcor (AL-cohr). Can you see Alcor?

The Science Behind the Fun

By finding one group of stars, you can find many more in the sky. This is a great way to start to learn where things are! Did you notice some stars had a little color? Look at orange-colored Betelgeuse and Aldebaran. Look at white-colored Sirius. The color actually means something. Star color tells you star temperature. Red and orange stars are the coolest, yellow and white stars are medium temperature, and blue-white and blue stars are the hottest. Now, these colors are not bright colors, so don't expect to see Betelgeuse looking like a bright red stop sign, but you can see a little bit of color. Are these colors surprising to you? We're used to using blue to represent cold and red to represent hot, but star colors are the opposite. Red means cool and blue means hot.

Aldebaran is the brightest star in the constellation of Taurus (TOR-us) the Bull. Sirius, the brightest star in our nighttime sky, is part of the constellation of Canis (CANE-nuhs) Major, the Big Dog. Procyon is part of the constellation of Canis Minor, the Little Dog.

See the Lion and the Queen in Spring

LAB 26

Time
10 minutes

Materials

- Your science notebook
- Pencil

Safety Tips and Setup Hints

- Be careful when you are outside looking at the sky. Make sure you are in a safe location. Wear reflective or light-colored clothing so people can see you.

- If you go out of town to a dark location, have an adult call the nonemergency phone number of the local police to let them know where you are and what you will be doing. Do not set up on private property without the property owner's permission. Follow all local laws. Beware that in many towns, parks close at sunset.

- If you are outside for a long time, you can get chilled, even when it isn't that cold. Dress in comfortable layers.

- These instructions work best in May.

Our Big Dipper can help us find even more star groups.

Instructions

Step 1: Go outside about an hour after sunset in May and face north. If you aren't sure which direction is north, then during the daytime, use Lab 3, "Determining Directions" (see page 16), or use a compass.

Step 2: Look up. The Big Dipper will be hanging "upside down" above you. The bowl of the Big Dipper will be on the left, and the crooked handle will be on the right. Now, turn around and face south. Look overhead. Now, the Big Dipper's bowl will be on the right and the handle will be on the left. Once you find it, sketch it in your notebook. (Fig. 1)

Step 3: Now, keep facing south. Imagine the bowl of the Big Dipper is filled with water. Poke a hole in the Dipper's bowl, and all the water falls out through the hole onto more stars. The right side of the group looks like a backward question mark—ʕ—and the left side looks like a small triangle. The backward question mark is the head and neck of Leo the Lion. The small triangle is Leo's back legs and tail. Once you find Leo, sketch him in your notebook. (Fig. 2)

Step 4: Next, turn around and face north again. Look for the Big Dipper. Draw a line through the two stars farthest from the handle to Polaris, the North Star. Keep going down and a little to the left until you see a W of stars. The W might be a bit sideways, so it could look a bit like this: ∑. This W is Cassiopeia the Queen. Make a sketch of Cassiopeia in your notebook. (If you live farther south, the Queen may be below the horizon and not visible.) (Fig. 3)

Creative Enrichment

Try to make your own planetarium. There are many ways to do it—but make sure an adult is there to help. Use constellation books or pictures online to choose your stars. Grab some paper cups and poke holes in the bottom to represent different constellations. Put a flashlight into the cup and shine the "stars" on the ceiling. Or, to make a bigger planetarium, use a large oatmeal container and a bright LED light or large flashlight. There are also directions and videos online to make your own planetarium dome! You can also make constellations using glow-in-the-dark stars or strings of holiday lights. Use your imagination to bring the night sky indoors!

The Science Behind the Fun

The Big Dipper can be a useful group of stars! Follow the two bowl stars to the North Star. Keep going to Cassiopeia. Follow the curve of the handle to Arcturus. Let the water in the bowl fall onto Leo the Lion. As long as you can find that Dipper, you have a good chance to find more!

As you learned in Lab 46, "Find the Dipper and the Pole in Spring" (see page 126), our Earth's North Pole points almost right at Polaris. As the Earth turns, everything seems to turn around the North Star. Now, depending on where you live, you may notice some of the stars right around that Pole star never set. The farther north you go, Polaris is higher and higher in the sky and more stars in the sky never seem to set. When you are right at the North Pole, all the stars seem to turn around Polaris and none of them set. The farther south you go, Polaris is lower and lower, and fewer stars around Polaris never set. Right at the Earth's equator, all the stars rise and set. If you keep going south, you can't see Polaris anymore because it is below the horizon. You may wonder if the Earth's South Pole points to a "South Star." No, there is no South Star. The fact that we have a star in the spot where the North Pole points is just by chance. If you are south of the equator and you want to try to find where the South Pole points, some people use a constellation called the Southern Cross. The bottom of the cross points toward where the south sky pole would be, a little farther away.

Fig. 1: Go outside and find the Dipper.

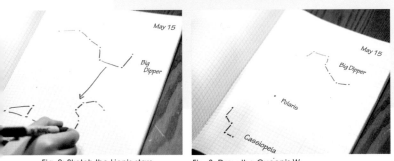

Fig. 2: Sketch the Lion's stars.

Fig. 3: Draw the Queen's W.

More Resources

Do you want to continue the astronomy fun? Many resources are in your town or online. Here are some suggestions:

- The best way to learn the sky is to keep trying! Go out as often as you can, and keep observing, sketching, and taking notes. Watch the Moon during the day and at night. Watch the constellations from month to month. Look for sunrise and sunset. Try to get out to a dark sky spot when you can. Look back at your notes from time to time and see how much you have learned. Do this before you buy a telescope. It can be easier to use a telescope when you first know what you are looking at.

- Visit your local planetarium or science museum. Many of them have programs to show you what is in tonight's night sky, and this program changes all year long as the seasons change and you can see different stars. Some of them also have night sky telescope programs.

- Visiting a planetarium might be a good idea to do before you try Labs 21 through 26. It's also a good idea if you want to learn how to find Mercury, Venus, Mars, Jupiter, or Saturn in the night sky. Earth moves and these planets move, so they are not in the same part of the sky every year and they can be harder to learn.

- Find out if your local planetarium or science museum offers camp or overnight programs, or find out what age you need to be to volunteer there.

- Find a local astronomy club. Many of them have programs that anyone can go to, and the members may even set up telescopes after the meeting. Other clubs set up telescopes in public locations. Walk up and take a look!

- Look for astronomy podcasts online or in an app store.

- Some local libraries have telescopes or binoculars you can check out for a few weeks. Try before you buy!

- Look for stargazing or "star party" activities at parks, museums, and planetariums. Many times, these events happen when there are interesting things happening in the sky, such as eclipses or meteor showers.

- There are many ways you can help do real science! Search for "citizen science" programs online, such as:
  - Zooniverse: www.zooniverse.org
  - NASA S'COOL Rover Cloud Observations program: scool.larc.nasa.gov

- Want to know what is going on in the Universe? Check out NASA's website, www.nasa.gov, or the European Space Agency's website, www.esa.int.

- If you need to find out your local time for sunrise, sunset, moonrise, and moonset, or if you need to find out Moon phases, go to the U.S. Naval Observatory's website: aa.usno.navy.mil.

- There are many different space telescopes that NASA has to look at nearby and faraway things in the Universe:
  - Spitzer Space Telescope: www.spitzer.caltech.edu
  - Hubble Space Telescope: www.hubblesite.org
  - Chandra X-Ray Observatory: chandra.harvard.edu
  - Fermi Gamma-ray Space Telescope: fermi.gsfc.nasa.gov

- Want to learn more about Mars? Visit mars.jpl.nasa.gov.

- Download and use free computer planetarium software, such as:
  - Stellarium: www.stellarium.org
  - WorldWide Telescope: www.worldwidetelescope.org

- You can take your own pictures of things in the night sky using MicroObservatory: www.cfa.harvard.edu/smg/website/own.

- There is something interesting in the sky every night. Find out where to look at www.earthsky.org/tonight.

Acknowledgments

So many people have assisted me with this book and I would like to acknowledge them here, though my thanks will never be enough in return for all the help they gave me. First and foremost, thank you to my husband, Brian, who encouraged me throughout this entire process, and thanks to my entire family.

Thanks are due to all the staff at Quarry Books and all the editors and designers for their patience, kindness, and enthusiasm. Jonathan Simcosky, you and your fellow staff took a chance on a rookie author, and for that, I am grateful.

I must acknowledge the beautiful work of my photographer, David Miller. You made these activities shine like no one else could.

Thank you to all the moms and dads (most especially Kelli Landes, Joe Kim, and Glenn and Barb Yehling) who agreed to allow their children to appear in photos for this book—and a huge thanks to the kids, too!

Finally, thank you to all of the hundreds of staff, past and present, I have worked with at the Adler Planetarium. You all have inspired me to be a better educator.

I hope this book makes all of you proud!

About the Author

Michelle Nichols is Master Educator at the Adler Planetarium in Chicago, Illinois, where she has worked for more than twenty years. She earned a bachelor of science degree from the University of Illinois at Urbana-Champaign and a master of education degree from National-Louis University. Michelle is an avid night sky watcher, and she also loves to run, cook, garden, and cheer on her favorite Chicago sports teams. She lives in the suburbs of Chicago with her husband.

Thank You!

Matthew

Kathryn

Darwin

Novella

Madison

Claudia

Mikayla

Arlo

Analise

Ruby

Logan

Elio

Elijah

Glossary

asteroid—An object in space made of rock and metal (and sometimes ice) that goes around the Sun.

atmosphere—Air

cardinal directions—North, south, east, and west.

comet—An object in space that is mostly made of ice and rock.

constellation—A group of stars in a shape or pattern.

crater—A hole made in an object when something from space smashes into it.

crystal—A hard material made of small bits that are in patterns and interesting shapes. Crystals can look like cubes, needles, tubes, or many other shapes. Table salt, quartz, and diamonds are examples of crystals.

diameter—How wide something is.

dwarf planet—An object that is smaller than a planet, round, and orbits the Sun. Some scientists call Pluto a dwarf planet.

Earth's axis—A line from the Earth's north pole to its south pole through the center of Earth.

eclipse—When one object blocks the light from another object.

equator—The line that separates an object into a north half and a south half.

fall equinox—The first day of fall. One of two days during the year when the Sun rises exactly in the east and sets exactly in the west.

frequency—The number of light waves or light rays that travel past a single spot in one second.

galaxy—A huge system of millions or billions of stars, planets, and other objects. Our home galaxy is called the Milky Way.

gamma rays—A type of light that our eyes cannot see. Gamma rays have shorter wavelengths than X-rays. Gamma rays have the shortest wavelengths so they can pass right through different objects. Gamma rays that strike the human body can harm the small bits that our cells are made of.

height—How tall something is.

hematite—A reddish-gray or silver-gray material partly made of iron.

horizon—The line where the sky appears to meet the ground.

infrared light (or infrared rays)—A type of light that our eyes cannot see. Infrared light has a longer wavelength than visible light. Some animals, like snakes, can see some types of infrared light.

latitude—A line on the Earth that shows how far north or south of the equator a place is.

length—How long something is.

lens—A curved piece of see-through material, such as glass or plastic, that causes light to bend, or travel in a different direction.

local noon—The time when the Sun is highest in the sky in a day for a location. This time does not always happen at 12 noon according to a clock.

longitude—A line drawn from the Earth's north pole to the Earth's south pole through the Earth's equator.

lunar eclipse—When the Moon passes through the Earth's shadow in space. If you were standing on the Moon, the Earth would block the light from the Sun.

meteor—A chunk of rock or metal in space.

meteorite—A chunk of rock or metal from space that has hit the ground.

meteoroid—A chunk of rock or metal from space that is moving through the air.

microwave light (or microwaves)—A type of light that our eyes cannot see. Microwave light has a longer wavelength than infrared light. An example of microwave light is the energy that microwave ovens create that is used to cook food.

Milky Way—The name of our galaxy. Also, a name of the faint cloudy-looking, or "milky," band of stars that can sometimes be seen in the night sky.

mineral—Any material that isn't made by something that is alive.

Moon—Our Earth's natural satellite.

Moon phase—The amount of the lit part of the Moon that can be seen from the Earth.

North Pole—The north end of the axis of the Earth.

North Star—The star closest to the place in the sky that the Earth's North Pole points to. Right now, Polaris is the North Star.

opaque—An object that is not see-through & that light cannot pass through. Concrete is an example.

optical illusion—When you see something that is not actually there, or when something looks different from normal.

orbit—When one object goes around another object.

planet—A large round object in space that orbits the Sun. Many scientists call Mercury, Venus, Earth, Mars, Jupiter, Saturn, Uranus, and Neptune planets, and others include Pluto and other objects as planets.

prism—An object that breaks, or separates, light into its colors.

radio light (or radio waves)—A type of light that our eyes cannot see. Radio light (or radio waves) has a longer wavelength than microwave light. An example of radio light is the signals that televisions receive.

rainbow—All of the colors that make up the light from our Sun. Also, an arch of colors in the sky made of the colors of light from our Sun.

revolve—To orbit, or to go around, an object.

rotate—To turn, or spin, around in a circle.

rust—A red or orange coating made when the mineral iron reacts with water and oxygen.

satellite—An object that goes around, or orbits, another object. Satellites can be "natural" or "artificial." Natural satellites are moons. Artificial satellites are objects made by people that are sent into space.

solar eclipse—When the Moon passes in front of the Sun and blocks the light from the Sun, as seen from the Earth.

solar system—Our Sun and all the objects around and near our Sun.

South Pole—The south end of the axis of the Earth.

spacecraft—An object or robot made by people and sent into space.

speed of light—How fast light travels through empty space, or about 186,000 miles (300,000 kilometers) per second.

spring equinox—The first day of spring. One of two days during the year when the Sun rises exactly in the east and sets exactly in the west.

star—A large object in space that is bigger than planets and makes its own energy.

stratosphere—The layer of our Earth's air above the troposphere. This is also the layer where jet airplanes often fly.

summer solstice—The first day of summer. Also the day when the Sun appears highest in the sky.

Sun—Our star. Our Sun is the only star in our solar system.

sunrise—When the Sun appears to move from below the horizon up into the sky.

sunset—When the Sun appears to move from the sky to below the horizon.

telescope—A tool used to make faraway objects look closer.

thermometer—A tool used to measure temperature.

transit—When one object passes in front of another, but the object is too small to completely block the other.

translucent—An object where some, but not all, light can completely pass through it. An example is tissue paper.

transparent—An object where light can completely pass through it. An example is glass.

troposphere—The layer of our Earth's air where most of our weather happens; this is also the layer of air closest to the ground.

ultraviolet light (or ultraviolet rays)—A type of light that our eyes cannot see. Ultraviolet light has a shorter wavelength than visible light. An example of ultraviolet light is the type of light that gives us a tan. Another type of ultraviolet light can damage part of our skin, giving us a sunburn. Some animals, such as bees, can see some ultraviolet light.

Universe—Everything everywhere that we can see.

visible light—Light or energy that our eyes can see.

wavelength—How scientists measure light. Light travels as waves, and the size of one of these waves is a wavelength. Light that is in a certain range of wavelengths can be seen by our eyes. Light that is not within that range cannot be seen by our eyes.

weathering—When an object breaks into smaller bits due to water, weather, ice, waves, and changes in temperature. Objects can also be "weathered" if they are hit by smaller objects over a long time.

weight—How heavy something is.

width—How wide something is.

winter solstice—The first day of winter. Also the day when the Sun appears lowest in the sky.

X-rays—A type of light that our eyes cannot see. X-ray light has a shorter wavelength than ultraviolet light. X-rays have such a short wavelength that they can sometimes travel through our bodies. Doctors can use the X-ray light that travels through our bodies and the X-rays that are absorbed by our bones to create a picture of our insides.

Index